Cross-Stitch Samplers

JANE KENDON

Cross-Stitch Samplers

St. Martin's Press
New York

Library of Congress Cataloging in Publication Data

Kendon, Jane.
    Cross-stitch samplers.

    1. Cross-stitch-Patterns. 2. Samplers.
I. Batsford, B. T. II. Title.
TT778.C76K45 1986   746.3   86-3804
ISBN 0-312-17681-3

Printed in Great Britain

Published in Great Britain in
1986 by B.T. Batsford Ltd.

Contents

Acknowledgements

Firstly I must thank family and friends for their help and support during the writing of this book. In particular I thank my mother, Helen Kendon, and my brother and sisters Samuel, Trudy and Sally who took most of the strain!

My thanks also to Gill Wyatt-Smith of the Yew Tree Gallery, Ellastone, Derbyshire, for kindly allowing me to make an analysis of her great-grandmother's sampler for the chapter on designing samplers.

Last but not least I would thank Nancy Hill, Margery Sharratt, and Rhys Brookes for their sterling efforts on my behalf.

Foreword

At a recent exhibition of my sampler designs many people asked me to write a book on the making and designing of cross stitch samplers. The beauty of cross stitch is that although it can look extremely complex and intricate it is in fact very easy to sew. Sewing cross stitch is a logical and methodical discipline, but it is also flexible, so that simple designs can be made to look effective.

The cross stitch sampler is one of the best-known forms of embroidery and yet sampler design seems to have been neglected a little in the past few decades. I hope through this book to show that anyone of any age can sew and design their own sampler, and in a small way further the revival of interest in this type of embroidery. To my mind what makes a sampler so distinctive from other sorts of embroidery is its characteristic form and content. Samplers are personalized embroideries, where the embroiderer is creating not just a beautiful picture, but also something very individual.

As with so many creative activities, the problem with sewing and designing samplers can be knowing just how and where to begin. This book gives a few basic principles and some practical advice for the whole procedure of making and designing samplers. In the first chapter there is step-by-step advice on the basic cross stitch, the materials needed and the reading of charts. Chapter 3 deals with designing samplers and gives advice on colour, content and form.

The book contains both charted samplers and a reference chapter to help you when designing your own sampler. The designs are charted on graph paper, and thus each stitch can be easily counted on to an evenweave fabric. The designs vary in degree of difficulty and there are notes with each design to guide the embroiderer. If you feel confident about your ability to sew cross stitch then you may wish to pass straight on to the charted designs (Chapter 2), or indeed to the chapter on the designing of samplers.

The designs could also be sewn in canvas work, though that is not the subject of this book.

1 SEWING CROSS STITCH SAMPLERS

Originally samplers were pieces of embroidery used to record stitches and sewing techniques that were then passed down the generations. As pattern books began to appear, the function of samplers as a source of reference was removed and so they came to be used more as an educational and decorative exercise. These are the samplers which are best known today, sewn toward the end of the eighteenth and during the nineteenth centuries. Small girls (and boys) sewed them, and often put events such as coronations, marriages, births and even deaths into their samplers.

Although the samplers used mainly cross stitch, they sometimes incorporated other stitches such as satin stitch and back stitch, and were sewn on the finest of fabrics. Those embroiderers must have needed much skill and patience, for ones so young! My own grandfather remembers how as children, he and his brothers and sisters were required to darn or sew samplers on Sundays to keep them quiet and occupied. Indeed, I have a tiny sampler worked by my great-grandfather in 1868 when he was six. Today, because cross stitch is so simple and because encouraging results can be achieved with only a little skill, it is still a good introduction to sewing for children.

Cross stitch embroidery is particularly appealing, as there is only the one basic stitch to learn. It is sewn on to a fabric (rather than an openweave canvas, as with canvas work), so there is no background to work. The materials required are few and with careful selection the expense can be kept to a minimum.

Materials

The fabric for the cross stitch samplers comes in various stitch counts and widths. It is often very wide and a number of samplers can be fitted on one full width. You can cut the cost by putting the design sideways on the fabric, or by sharing the fabric with friends. Most craft shops or craft sections of department stores will have a selection of different fabrics to choose from. The most popular and available fabrics are aida, linen, hardanger and evenweave, all of which come in various colours and stitch sizes.

These fabrics are ones where the warp and weft threads are continuous across the length and width of the fabric and which have the same number of threads to 2.5 cm (1 in.) in both directions. You will need to know this number

so that you can work out how large the finished design will be and thus how much fabric to buy. I would strongly recommend that the less experienced embroiderer does not use a fabric that has more than 11 stitches to 2.5 cm (1 in.). Do make sure that the fabric you buy is evenly woven, as an unevenly woven fabric is much more difficult to sew. Do not use an openweave fabric such as canvas unless you intend to sew the sampler in canvas work. Fig. 1 shows a few of the different fabrics and their respective stitch counts. The same symbol has been sewn on each of the fabrics to show how the different stitch counts affect the size of a design.

The thread used in sewing cross stitch samplers is usually stranded cotton (sometimes referred to as silks, or in the USA as six strand embroidery floss). There are many different makes and hundreds of colours to choose from. Make sure the thread you use is colourfast. The stranded cotton is made up of six fine strands. A varying number of strands is used according to the size of weave of the fabric, and the size of each stitch. Table 1 lists the usual number of strands used for the various fabric stitch counts. However, do try out the threads on your chosen fabric before you start sewing. The stitches usually look best when the holes of the fabric are filled without losing the definition of the cross. If you think you will need more than one skein of a particular colour, buy more at the same time, as the threads can vary between dye lots.

You will need blunt-ended tapestry needles. These push the fabric fibres apart, whereas a sharp-ended needle will split the fibres. A size 24 is suitable for most fabrics.

Table 1: Number of strands of thread used for different fabric stitch counts, and needle size

no. of stitches to 2.5 cm (1 in.)	no. of strands of thread	size of needle (tapestry)
9	3	24
11	2/3	24
14	2	24/26
18	1/2	26
22	1	26

1. An assortment of different fabrics:

(a) white hardanger 22 to 2.5 cm (1 in.);
(b) ivory aida 18 to 2.5 cm (1 in.);
(c) ivory fine linen 29 to 2.5 cm (1 in.) worked over two;
(d) white aida 14 to 2.5 cm (1 in);
(e) beige crash 26 to 2.5 cm (1 in.) worked over two;
(f) beige aida 11 to 2.5 cm (1 in.);
(g) white coarse linen 18 to 2.5 cm (1 in.) worked over two;
(h) beige evenweave 28 to 2.5 cm (1 in.) worked over three.

You will also need:

- sticky tape;
- small embroidery scissors;
- sewing/machine cotton for neatening fabric edges;
- pencil and eraser;
- protective material to keep your sampler clean.

Preparing to sew

If you are a beginner to cross stitch embroidery, then work a small piece of material before choosing one of the simpler designs. Otherwise choose a design according to your confidence or ambition! There are notes with each design which estimate the degree of difficulty and will help you to decide which design to sew. Each design has calculations for the approximate size of the design on various different fabrics. If the fabric you wish to use is not included in the list, either approximate to the stitch count nearest yours or make a new calculation. (To do this, refer to 'Calculations' in Chapter 3.) Remember that

2. Marking the centre stitch lines on the fabric.

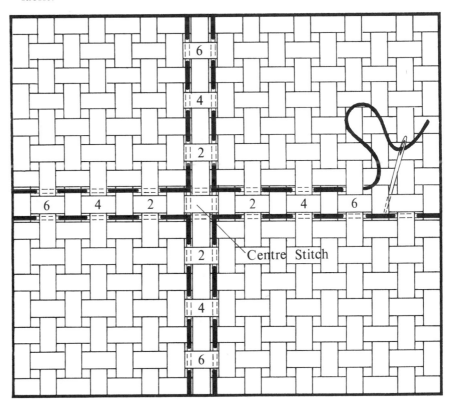

the fewer the number of stitches to 2.5 cm (1 in.), the bigger the final design, and thus the more fabric that is required. Allow at least 7.5 cm (3 in.) on all four sides for turnings and margins. Always err on the generous side.

If the fabric has not been cut on the straight when you buy it, then pull a thread across the width and cut across. Measure off the required amount and cut along the thread lines. Neaten the edges of the fabric by overcasting by hand, or use a machine zig-zag stitch. Using a damp cloth, iron any folds and creases out of the fabric before you start sewing. Inspect the fabric carefully to see if it has any marks on it. Quite often you will find that the fabric has become a little dirty down the fold line. Try to avoid using this if you can, and use the side of the fabric that has been folded to the inside.

How much marking of reference lines you do is really a matter of personal choice. If you have any experience of reading from a chart or if you are doing a small design you may find that only a little marking is necessary. However, the beginner will find it helpful to mark the centre stitch lines both horizontally and vertically. To do this, fold the fabric in half, and using an ordinary sewing thread, sew a running stitch (the same length as each cross stitch) the length of the fabric. Sew on both sides of the centre stitch. Do the same for the width but work from the centre (Fig. 2).

Sewing technique

Cross stitch is extremely simple to sew, but do try a few practice stitches on a spare piece of fabric before starting to work a sampler design. Use Table 1 to decide how many strands of thread to use with which fabric. Always use a short length of thread of about 60 cm (24 in.), or less if you find it easier. It is not necessary to use an embroidery frame when sewing a sampler (unless you are using woollen yarn), but many people prefer to use one. A frame does tend to keep the stitching nice and even. If you have a frame it is probably best to try a few stitches with and without and see which suits you best. Personally, I rarely use a frame and find that any creases or unevenness in tension are pulled out when the embroidery is stretched.

If you decide to use a frame you will use the stab-stitch method of sewing; that is, straight up and straight down in two separate moves. You can also use this method if you are not using a frame. Alternatively, you can slip the needle straight from hole to hole, which makes for much quicker sewing and helps to keep your place on the fabric. This is the method I usually use (Fig. 6).

When you begin sewing, hold a short length at the end of the thread against the wrong side of the fabric. The first few diagonal stitches will hold it in place against the back of the fabric. Later, slip the thread behind other stitches to secure it wherever possible. This method of starting a thread should in particular be used if you are sewing a sampler for competition or exhibition purposes, or if you are using a thick thread such as a woollen yarn as it gives a smoother finish. However, it is not always an easy or possible way to secure the thread, and for many people it is easier to start by tying a knot in the end of the thread and slipping the needle through behind the knot (Fig. 3). The

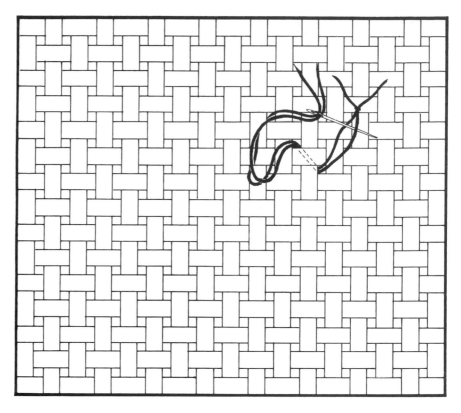

3. Starting a thread using a knotted end.

4. Sewing a cross stitch over a single thread of fabric.

5. Sewing a cross stitch over two threads of fabric.

disadvantage with this method is that the knots occasionally come undone.

When you have secured the end of the thread follow the letters in Fig. 4, up through **A**, down through **B**, etc. This sequence must be followed if you are sewing over a single thread. However if you are sewing over two threads or using aida fabric then the single cross stitch can be sewn as in Fig. 5. This is a slightly quicker method, as the needle can be slipped straight across from **B** to **C**.

You will notice that the top diagonal in the diagrams runs from top left to bottom right. It does not matter which way they run, but all top stitches should run in the same direction. If you are left-handed you may well find that the other direction is easier. Find out which suits you best by sewing a few practice stitches. If as a beginner you find you have done a whole section (or the odd stitch) in the wrong direction, do not unpick them. Unpicking is a little disheartening and is not really necessary in this case. Mistakes can easily happen, especially as the fabric is turned round. You may find it helps to mark

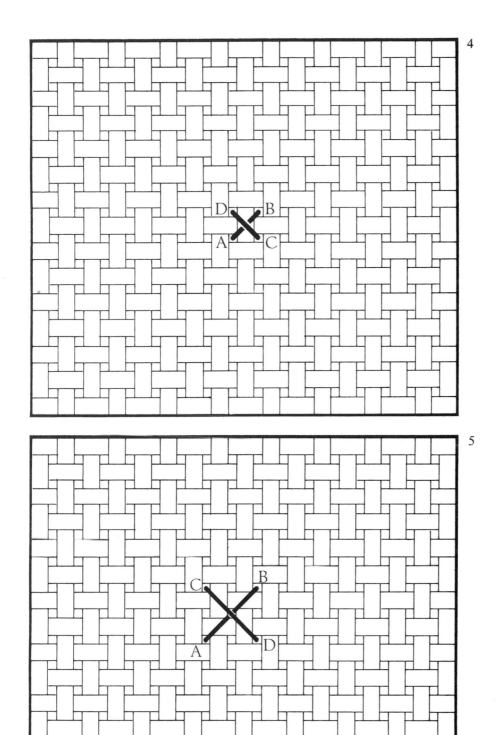

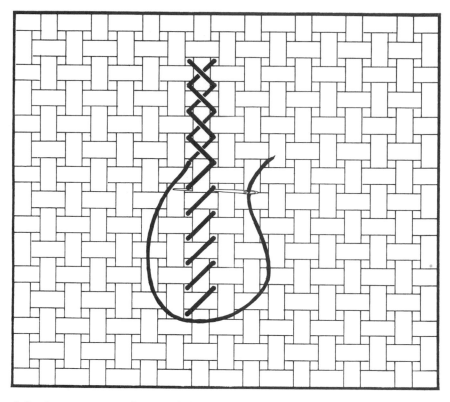

6. Sewing a sequence of cross stitches.

the top of the fabric with a brightly coloured thread. However, if you are sewing a sampler for competition or exhibition then all the top stitches must run in the same direction.

Stitches which are separate from others or are on a diagonal should be sewn individually, whereas a row of the same colour stitches should be sewn first all one way and then crossed back over in sequence (Fig. 6).

It is often better to catch a thread behind other threads on the back of a design, rather than continually stopping and starting. So if you wish to sew stitches of a particular colour which are a few stitches apart, catch the thread behind under other stitches. However, try not to run the thread directly behind the fabric as some dark and bright colours may show through.

Having finished a length of thread, pull it through to the back and slip it under a few stitches to keep it firmly in place. Clip the thread close to the fabric to keep the back as neat and tidy as possible.

Working the design

By now you will have decided on your design, collected and prepared your fabric, and done a small practice piece, so you know how many threads to use of the stranded cotton. On the charts each square represents one cross stitch and each different symbol represents a different colour, as denoted in the key.

Knowing how and where to start a design is always the most difficult part, but the more you sew of a design the easier it becomes. There are two basic approaches when starting to sew a design. The first method is to place the central symbols (that is, to start at the centre) and then work outwards. The second is to count out very carefully from the centre to a part of the border that runs right round the design. Note the number in pencil on the chart and carefully count out the same number from the centre, on to your fabric. It helps to mark the number off in tens using pins so that it can be easily checked. Now carefully sew the border in, counting and checking with the chart.

I would recommend the second method of starting a design, as you will find out at the earliest possible moment whether you have positioned the design correctly on the fabric, and indeed that you have cut the fabric to the right size. Once you have got this part of the design sewn the rest will fall into place much more easily. Choose symbols or patterns in the sampler that connect or relate closely to each other, rather than a symbol here and there. As you sew you will find the counting and placing becomes easier as the number of reference points increases.

Mistakes!

Everyone makes mistakes, especially when trying to position motifs correctly. It is important that the initial outline you sew is put in exactly the right place, as mistakes at this stage only compound one another later. If you go wrong, find out exactly where and unpick carefully to that point. When unpicking, put as little strain as possible on the fabric so as not to pull the fabric threads out of line or enlarge the holes. Keep the thread very short by cutting it frequently, so you only pull out short strands. Before you re-start sewing, go over the area that has been unpicked with sticky tape, so that all traces of thread are removed. Then cut a new piece of thread and re-sew.

Placing initials, names and dates

On many of the designs included in this book (and perhaps on your own sampler designs) you may wish to insert initials, names and dates. Jot down on a piece of paper the lettering and numbers that you wish to use, plus any punctuation. Find or design appropriate lettering, and sketch out the letters and numbers with the desired spacing on to graph paper (some is included at the end of this book). Take into account the amount of space provided on the design, and make sure the number of spaces needed comes within those available. Having counted the spaces both for the lettering and on the design, find the centre points by dividing in two. Sketch in the letters and numbers on the chart starting from the centre and working out (Fig. 7).

If you have an even number of spaces you will have to position the lettering

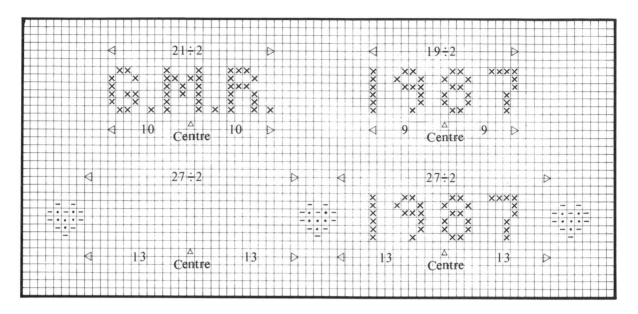

7. Placing letters and numbers on a
   chart.

slightly to one side or the other. If there is space remaining, due for instance to a
short date, then fill the empty spaces with symbols taken from Chapter 5 of this
book.

2 CHARTED SAMPLER DESIGNS

The following pages contain charted samplers of varying subject matter, colour, style, size and degree of difficulty. Notes with each design will help you to decide if you feel able to tackle them. Suggestions are also made on where to begin sewing a design and how to continue, though these are by no means the only approach. You will find that I often suggest starting a design by counting out from the centre to a part of the border that runs right round the design. This method is a personal preference, and it is just as correct to start at the centre of the design and work outwards.

If a chart is fairly large it may be split over two or four pages so that it is big enough to read easily. The centres are marked, so that it should not prove difficult to follow. You may find that it helps to mark the centre stitch lines on your fabric (Fig. 2). Each coded square represents one cross stitch and its colour. The size of each design is given for the different stitch counts of the various fabrics. Each measurement has been rounded up to be on the safe side. If you decide to work a design at 22 stitches to 2.5 cm (1 in.), then halve the measurements given for 11 stitches to 2.5 cm (1 in.). Remember to add at least 15 cm (6 in.) to each measurement for margins and turnings when calculating how much fabric to purchase.

You need not, of course, use the thread colours I have selected, but if you decide to choose your own colours then I would suggest you first read the notes on colour in Chapter 3. I have used two strands of stranded cotton in all but the 'Anniversary Sampler' (where I have used one strand of Paterna Persian Yarn). I have given both Anchor and DMC thread colour numbers for the designs. It should be noted, however, that the designs were worked in Anchor threads, and the DMC alternative will not give exactly the same result.

Chapter 1 will help if you need guidance on the sewing technique, reading of charts, or placing of initials and dates. Otherwise, once you have finished your sampler, proceed to Chapter 4 on how to finish, stretch and frame it.

As well as the full-size samplers, there are also four small designs taken from four of the larger ones. These make charming little pictures and are quick and simple to sew. They make an excellent introduction to sewing cross stitch samplers for the beginner. If you are at all hesitant about your ability to sew one of the larger designs then try the smaller extract first. When you have succeeded in sewing that, you may well find that you feel able to tackle the larger design. You can, of course, choose your own extracts from the various designs and sketch them on to a piece of graph paper. The repetition of a single motif with a simple border placed round it can look most attractive.

The Garden Sampler

Here is a design for anyone who loves gardens, and especially for those who like working in the garden. This design comes from one I did for some gardening friends of mine who were getting married. I believe it is much appreciated, as it takes pride of place in their overgrown sitting-room! The colours are rich and colourful and give a very warm impression.

The inner frame has been left empty so that you can insert your own verse or motto. You could put in the verse I have used in 'A Garden Verse'; this will fit the frame. Alternatively, if you were sewing the design for a present, you could put the recipient's name in the frame with an appropriate date.

Although this is not a difficult design to sew, it does not have the advantage of a border line running right round the design, as so many of my samplers have. For this reason I would suggest that you find the centre and count up to the lower edge of the inner frame, and sew this in first. Then sew in part of the tree and the line of little flowers. Count out from the end of the line of flowers to the border, and stitch up the border until you can do a cross-reference with the brown inner frame. If you find you have placed the motifs correctly this far, then the remainder will be easy. Overall this is a fairly simple design with comparatively few motifs, and it should not take long to sew. The last colour to be sewn should, wherever possible, be white, so that it does not get dirty.

Design size: 107 × 139 squares.

stitch count	approx. size (cm)	approx. size (in.)
11	24.5 × 32	$9\frac{3}{4} \times 12\frac{3}{4}$
14	19.5 × 25	$7\frac{3}{4} \times 10$
18	15 × 19.5	$6 \times 7\frac{3}{4}$

Note: add 15 cm (6 in.) to each measurement for margins and turnings.
Fabric: beige aida 11 stitches to 2.5 cm (1 in.).

Key and thread numbers:

symbol	●	•	+	▲	−	○	△
colour	pink	lt green	brown	dk green	blue	white	yellow
Anchor	39	859	355	862	850	1	891
DMC	347	3052	975	935	926	BLANC	676

8. The Garden Sampler (see also colour
    plate 1).

symbol	colour
●	pink
●	lt green
○	brown
+	brown
◀	dk green
–	blue
○	white
△	yellow

A *Garden Verse*

This little design comes from the 'Garden Sampler'. Although the verse is simple, I am sure its sentiment is one that many people would agree with and be pleased to have in their home. The verse also fits the frame on the larger design.

Count out from the centre of the design to the brown part of the inner frame. Sew this in first, and the outer border should fit in easily. The technique of splitting the lettering into two colours can be used for any lettering. It looks very effective but is easy to sew.

The thread colours and colour coding are the same as those used for the main 'Garden Sampler' design.

Design size: 62 × 95 squares.

stitch count	approx. size (cm)	approx. size (in.)
11	14.5 × 22	$5\frac{3}{4} × 8\frac{3}{4}$
14	11.5 × 17	$4\frac{1}{2} × 6\frac{3}{4}$
18	9 × 13.5	$3\frac{1}{2} × 5\frac{1}{2}$

Note: add 15 cm (6 in.) to each measurement for margins and turnings.
Fabric: white aida 14 stitches to 2.5 cm (1 in.).

24

9. A Garden Verse.

1. A Garden Sampler

2. *A Wedding Sampler*

3. *Anniversary Sampler*

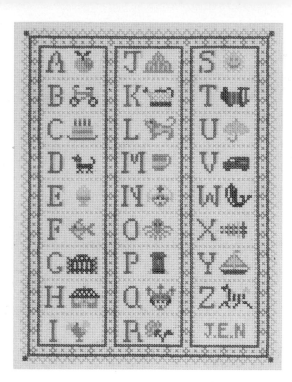

4. *Nursery Alphabet*

5. *Home Sweet Home*

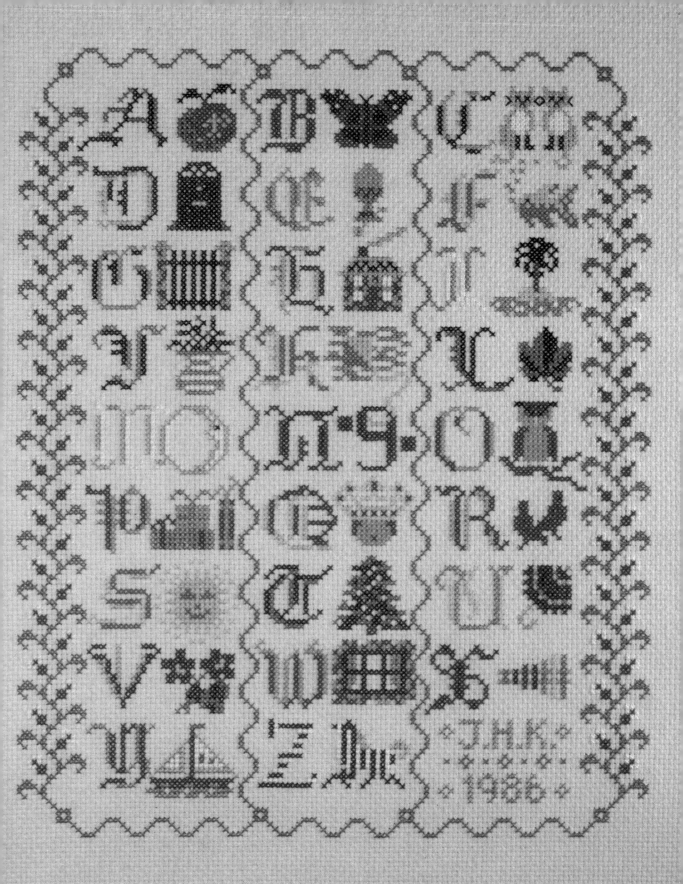

6. *An Illustrated Alphabet*

7. *African Sampler*

8. *Scandinavian Sampler*

9. A *Merry Christmas* Sampler

10. *Golden Days*

symbol	colour
△	yellow
−	blue
+	brown
●	lt green
●	pink

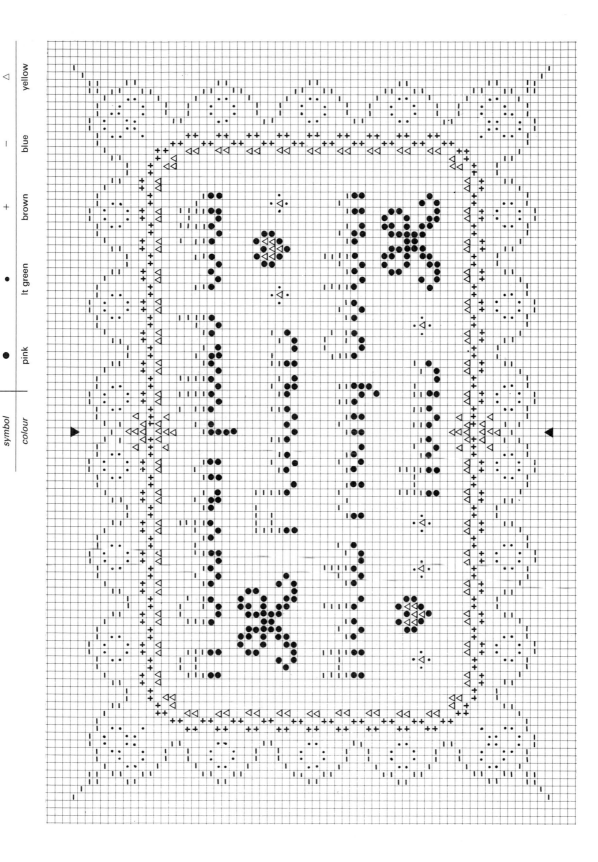

A Wedding Sampler

This sampler would make a lovely present for anyone who is getting married. The very first sampler I designed was for some friends of mine who were about to marry. They and their friends and relatives were so pleased with it that I decided to design a few more samplers, little knowing that it would lead eventually to the writing of this book! The love-birds, hearts and flowers make this a sampler that will soon become a treasured possession. The colours are soft and muted, and give the design an established look.

The sampler is not difficult to sew. The first task is to place the appropriate initials and dates in the spaces provided on the chart. The relevant alphabet and numbers are to be found in Chapter 5. Chapter 1 includes advice on how to place them. The most important thing is to sketch them in pencil and have an eraser handy! It always takes a few attempts to position the lettering correctly. If you have a very short date, fill the spaces with other motifs from Chapter 5. I have sewn the initials in red and beige, and the date in blue and yellow.

Start by finding the centre of the design and counting down to the red line at the bottom edge. Sew the red pattern all the way round the design, counting carefully and checking with any reference points you have marked in. Do not forget to leave the correct number of spaces for the bow at the top. The beige and blue parts of the border are easily sewn in next. Then place the bells, birds and pots of flowers, and the rest of the design should fit in easily.

Design size: 121 × 157 squares.

stitch count	approx. size (cm)	approx. size (in.)
11	27.5 × 36	$11 \times 14\frac{1}{2}$
14	22 × 28.5	$8\frac{3}{4} \times 11\frac{1}{4}$
18	17 × 22	$6\frac{3}{4} \times 8\frac{3}{4}$

Note: add 15 cm (6 in.) to each measurement for margins and turnings.
Fabric: ivory hardanger 22 stitches to 2.5 cm (1 in.), worked over two.

10. A Wedding Sampler (see also
colour plate 2).

Key and thread numbers:

symbol	●	–	●	▲	V	○
colour	red	blue	beige	brown	green	yellow
Anchor	338	849	831	898	860	887
DMC	922	926	7519	611	3052	3046

27

symbol	●	–	•	▲	V	○
colour	red	blue	beige	brown	green	yellow

symbol	●	−	•	▲	V	○
colour	red	blue	beige	brown	green	yellow

Anniversary Sampler

Although this sampler was designed specifically with wedding anniversaries in mind, it could also be used for other special celebrations. The strawberry border is a traditional feature of samplers, as are the alphabet and numbers. Unlike the other designs in this book, the sampler is sewn in woollen yarn. The colours are reminiscent of nineteenth-century samplers, and the yarn gives it a soft quality.

If you decide to sew the sampler in yarn, then it will need to be worked on an embroidery frame. It is a very simple design, and would be a good one for a comparative beginner to sew (particularly in stranded cotton). For the more experienced embroiderer, this design can be completed quickly, and thus be a useful present for when time is short.

Firstly, place the initials and dates in the spaces provided. (Chapter 1 gives advice on how to do this.) Use the numbers and letters included within the design. Begin sewing the sampler by finding the centre and counting out to the dark red inner border. Sew the zig-zag line first and then place the three dotted lines that go across the design. From these you should have little difficulty placing the other symbols. Once you have completed the inner border, start sewing the outer border using the inner one for constant reference. You may prefer to sew the dark green line that goes right round the design before you fill in the leaves and strawberries.

The Paterna Persian Yarn is available from NeedleArt House (see page 119). Use a single strand at a time, and sew the white in last, wherever possible, to keep it clean.

Design size: 111 × 139 squares.

stitch count	approx. size (cm)	approx. size (in.)
11	25.5 × 32	$10\frac{1}{4} × 12\frac{3}{4}$
14	20 × 25	8 × 10
18	15.5 × 19.5	$6\frac{1}{4} × 7\frac{3}{4}$

Note: add 15 cm (6 in.) to each measurement for margins and turnings.
Fabric: ivory aida 18 stitches to 2.5 cm (1 in.), worked over two.

11. Anniversary Sampler (see also
    colour plate 3).

Key and thread numbers:

symbol	☆	★	○	–	■	△	●	●	▲
colour	flesh	dk grey	lt grey	yellow	brown	white	green	dk pink	md pink
Paterna	874	210	212	704	413	260	601	275	211
Anchor	661	401	144	305	571	402	967	896	600

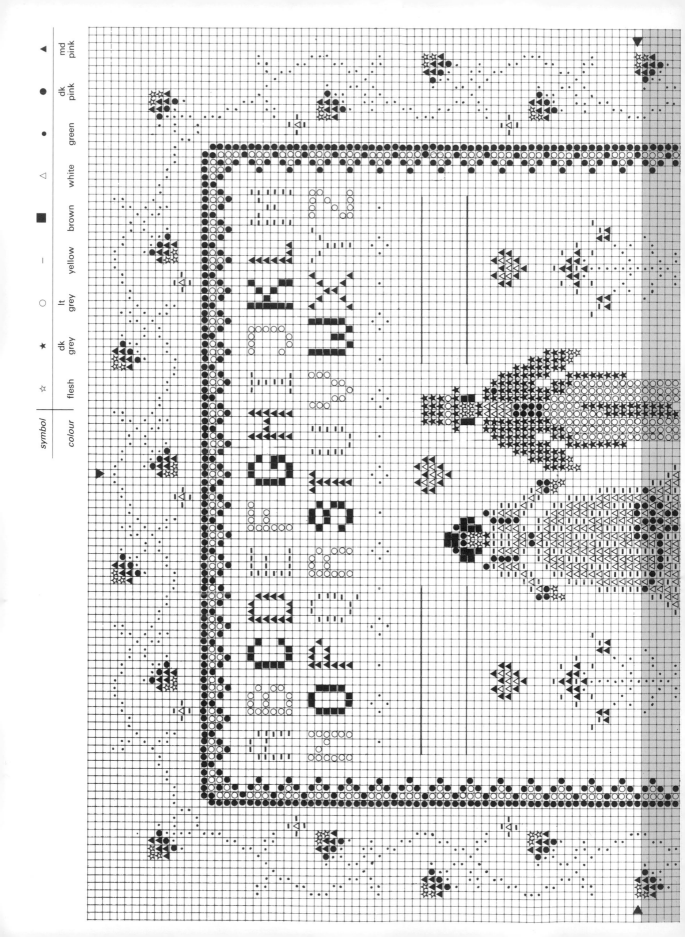

symbol	colour
☆	flesh
★	dk grey
○	lt grey
—	yellow
■	brown
△	white
•	green
●	dk pink
◀	md pink

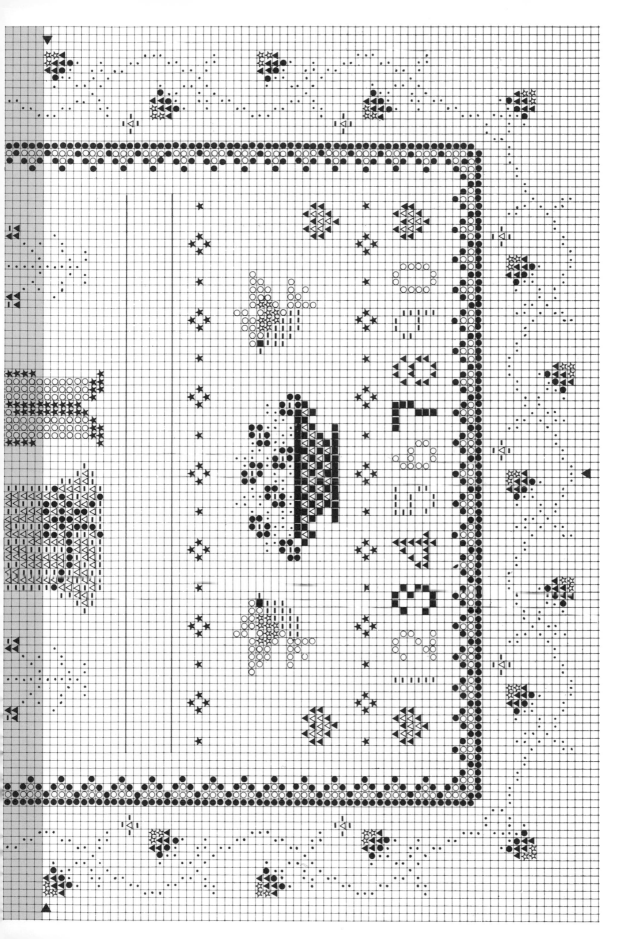

Nursery Alphabet and Nursery Numbers

These two samplers would brighten any child's room. The letters and symbols are clear and familiar and can help with learning alphabet and numbers. With jellies, trains, zebras and bicycles, the designs have a very light-hearted feel. The colours are bright and cheerful, in pretty pinks and greens, though I also think these designs would look particularly good in reds and blues. They would make super gifts for a young child or grandchild. Each design can of course stand on its own, but they also complement each other as a pair. (As the designs are similar, only the alphabet has been photographed.)

The designs are not difficult to sew and would be suitable for a younger or less experienced embroiderer. Start at the centre, and sew in the light green dotted lines first. These are easier to count than the solid dark green lines, as they are spaced apart. Count carefully, and check with other reference lines as you sew. When you have sewn the light green you should have lots of little boxes or panels to work within. Sewing in the letters will soon show if these have been put in correctly! Add the inner dark green lines only when you are sure the boxes and panels are correctly placed. Then sew the outer dark green lines and the light green zig-zag line. The motifs should be easy to position within the basic framework. I used the gold thread to sew the initials and dates, but you can of course choose whichever colour you wish.

If you would prefer to purchase the fabric and threads already chosen and cut to size then these designs can be bought as needlework kits, from Atlascraft Ltd (see page 119).

Design size (both samplers): 107 × 139 squares.

stitch count	approx. size (cm)	approx. size (in.)
11	24.5 × 32	$9\frac{3}{4} \times 12\frac{3}{4}$
14	19.5 × 25	$7\frac{3}{4} \times 10$
18	15 × 19.5	$6 \times 7\frac{3}{4}$

Note: add 15 cm (6 in.) to each measurement for margins and turnings.
Fabric: white aida 11 stitches to 2.5 cm (1 in.).

12. Nursery Alphabet (see also colour
    plate 4).

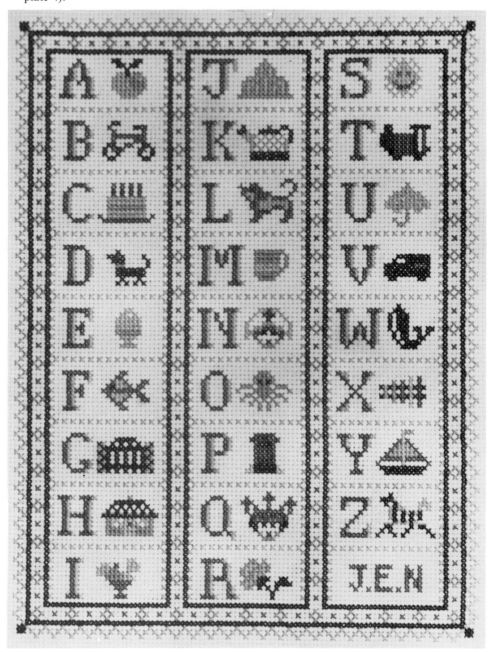

Key and thread numbers (both samplers):

symbol	◆	•	●	△	■	▲	○
colour	gold	lemon	dk green	lt green	grey	dk pink	lt pink
Anchor	307	301	210	206	400	38	50
DMC	783	676	910	966	414	335	605

symbol	colour
○	lt pink
▲	dk pink
■	grey
◁	lt green
●	dk green
·	lemon
◆	gold

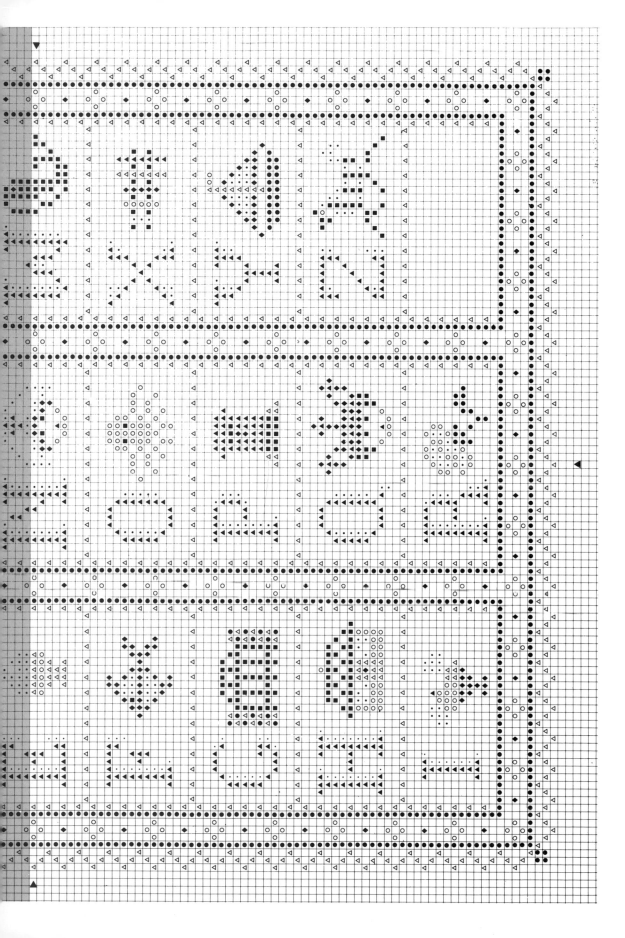

symbol	colour
○	lt pink
◀	dk pink
■	grey
◁	lt green
●	dk green
•	lemon
◆	gold

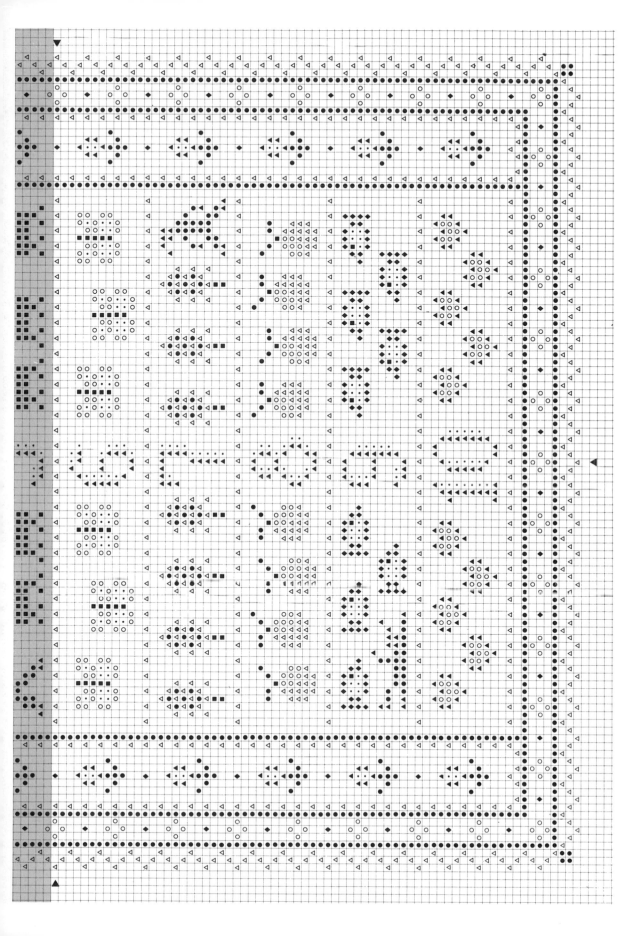

Home Sweet Home

'Home Sweet Home' must be the best-known of all sampler themes. As soon as samplers are mentioned people immediately think of the old, faded samplers they have seen. I have designed a sampler on the traditional theme, but using bright shades of pink, green and yellow. The sampler has a clean, fresh look that would be attractive hanging in an airy room, or brightening up a dark corner. The thatched cottage, butterflies and flowers all combine to make this a new variation on an old theme.

The outer and inner borders on this design give many reference points to sew by. Find the centre, count out to the beige inner border and sew this in first. Count carefully, checking with any reference lines you have put in. Once the inner border has been sewn in, the outer dark green border will be easy to place and complete. The border round the cottage needs a little time and care when placing it, as it is worked in an oval shape.

As the trees are not made up of regular repeated symbols you may find it easier to sew by working the light and dark green threads at once. To do this, thread up two needles with each of the greens. Sew a few stitches of each colour in turn, securing the colour that is not being used to one side (on the right side of the embroidery). The flowers in the baskets are intertwined, and look more complex than they are. If you sew in the mid-green stem first you should have no problems. The lettering should not present any difficulties, though you may prefer to work the two greens at once, as with the trees.

Design size: 107 × 137 squares.

stitch count	approx. size (cm)	approx. size (in.)
11	24.5 × 31.5	$9\frac{3}{4} \times 12\frac{1}{2}$
14	19.5 × 24.5	$7\frac{3}{4} \times 10$
18	15 × 19.5	$6 \times 7\frac{3}{4}$

Note: add 15 cm (6 in.) to each measurement for margins and turnings.
Fabric: ivory hardanger 22 stitches to 2.5 cm (1 in.), worked over two.

13. Home Sweet Home (see also colour
    plate 5).

Key and thread numbers:

symbol	▲	△	●	○	●	×
colour	dk yellow	lt yellow	dk green	md green	lt green	grey
Anchor	303	301	268	265	253	398
DMC	742	676	3345	471	472	415

symbol	—	V	■	9	■	☆
colour	lt pink	md pink	dk pink	violet	brown	beige
Anchor	24	27	29	108	355	368
DMC	776	899	891	211	975	437

symbol	colour
☆	beige
▲	brown
9	violet
■	dk pink
V	md pink
–	lt pink
×	grey
•	lt green
○	md green
●	dk green
△	lt yellow
▲	dk yellow

Just Home

I think 'Home Sweet Home' says so much to so many people that this small design, simple though it may be, would make a very welcome gift. The lettering comes from the main 'Home Sweet Home' sampler, and the design provides an excellent introduction to cross stitch work.

Count out from the centre and sew the beige inner border first. The outer border line should then fit in easily. The lettering can be placed with reference to the beige border, though you may like to work the two green threads at once, as described for the main 'Home Sweet Home' design.

The thread colours and colour coding are the same as for the large 'Home Sweet Home' sampler.

Design size: 55 × 95 squares.

stitch count	approx. size (cm)	approx. size (in.)
11	12.5 × 22	5 × 8¾
14	10 × 17	4 × 6¾
18	8 × 13.5	3¼ × 5½

Note: add 15 cm (6 in.) to each measurement for margins and turnings.
Fabric: white aida 11 stitches to 2.5 cm (1 in.).

46   14. Just Home.

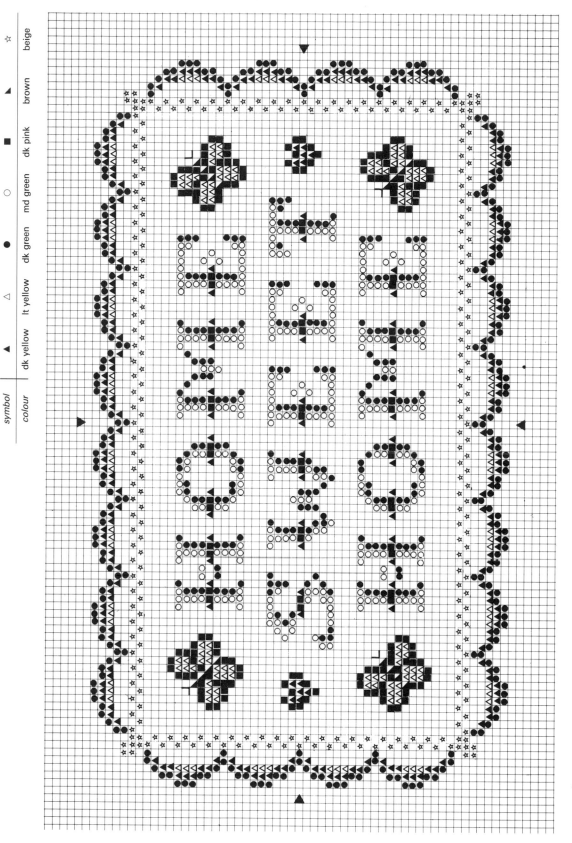

47

An Illustrated Alphabet

Alphabets are closely associated with sampler designs, so here is a sampler devoted solely to the alphabet: an illustrated alphabet. Each letter has a motif that is quite detailed and intricate in design. The colours are soft but rich and are sewn on to a beige fabric, giving the design a warm and homely feel. This sampler would make a suitable gift for anyone, of any age.

Although the design appears to be complex and detailed, it is in fact comparatively easy to sew. The mid-green border lines provide an excellent source of cross-reference, and once these have been completed the remainder is really quite easy, if a little time-consuming! So find the centre and count out the few stitches to the inner mid-green border line. Complete the border for the centre panel first, then sew in the borders for the two side panels. Then add the letters and motifs, working from the top and bottom to the centre, and checking carefully with the border lines as you sew.

I used blue for the initials and date, but you could of course choose any of the colours. If you would like to make the design a little brighter, then I would suggest you change the dark grey to black, and choose a brighter red, orange, yellow, blue and purple. The design could look very effective in these brighter colours. As ever, the choice of colour is very much a matter of personal choice.

Design size: 131 × 161 squares.

stitch count	approx. size (cm)	approx. size (in.)
11	30 × 37	12 × 14$\frac{3}{4}$
14	23.5 × 29	9$\frac{1}{2}$ × 11$\frac{1}{2}$
18	18.5 × 22.5	7$\frac{1}{2}$ × 9

Note: add 15 cm (6 in.) to each measurement for margins and turnings.
Fabric: beige aida 11 stitches to 2.5 cm (1 in.).

Key and thread numbers:

symbol	○	☆	1	◣	●	★
colour	white	beige	lt grey	brown	lt green	dk green
Anchor	1	347	398	351	876	879
DMC	BLANC	402	415	300	502	500

15. An Illustrated Alphabet (see also
    colour plate 6).

symbol	●	▲	8	△	−	■
colour	red	dk grey	orange	yellow	blue	purple
Anchor	20	401	339	891	920	873
DMC	347	535	920	676	932	315

symbol	○	☆	1	◣	•	★	●	▲	8	△	–	■
colour	white	beige	lt grey	brown	lt green	dk green	red	dk grey	orange	yellow	blue	purple

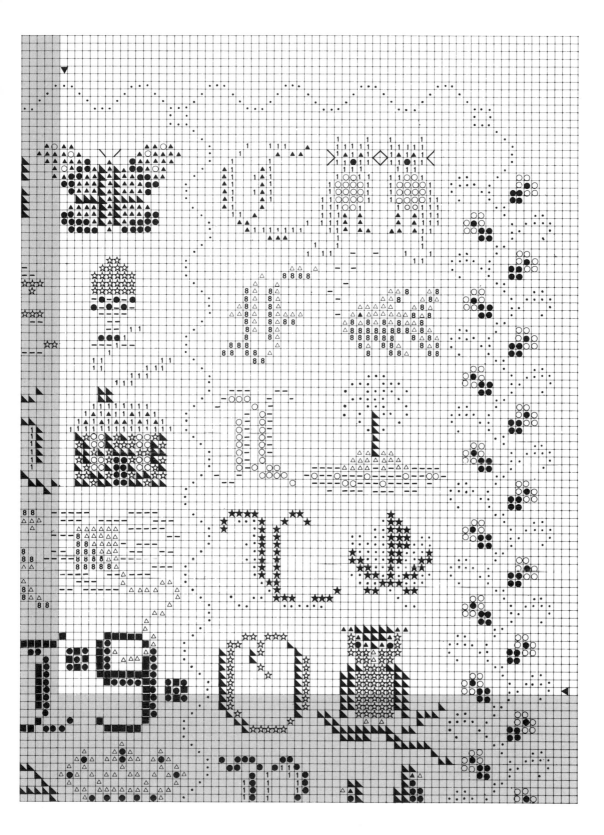

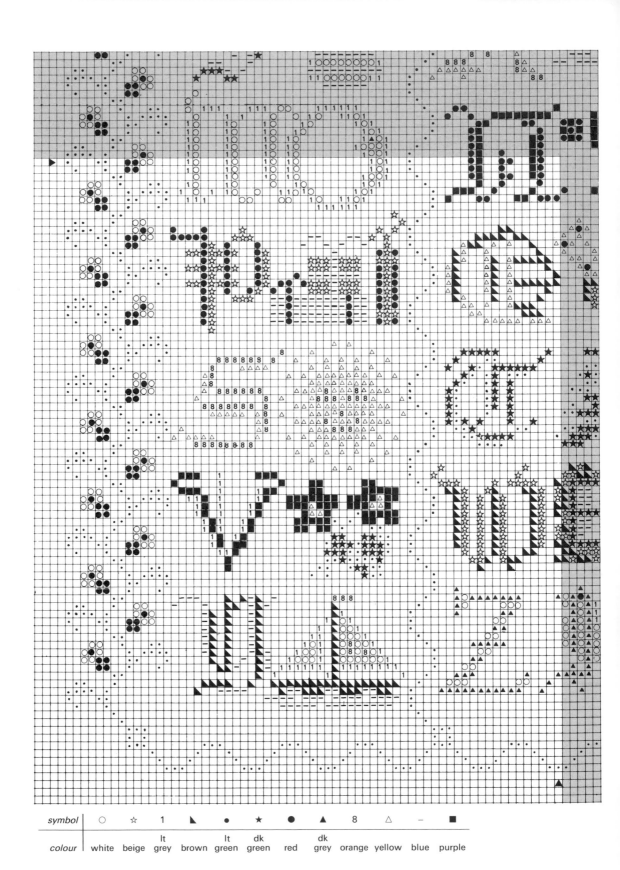

symbol	○	☆	1	◣	•	★	●	▲	8	△	–	■
colour	white	beige	lt grey	brown	lt green	dk green	red	dk grey	orange	yellow	blue	purple

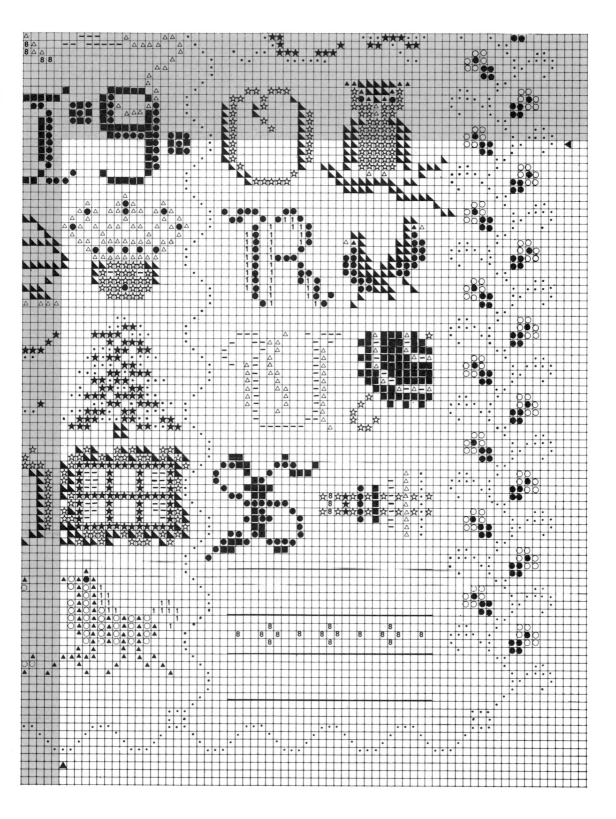

Cameo Letters

This little design would be just right to decorate some quiet corner. I have charted up just the border for the design so that you can choose whichever motif you like best from the main 'Illustrated Alphabet' design and fill it in. A pair or series of motifs would look very effective.

Find the centre of the design and count out to the border. Either sew in the green border complete with leaves, or just sew in the wavy mid-green line that goes right round the design. Then fill in the leaves, flowers and central motif.

The thread colours and colour coding are the same as for the main 'Illustrated Alphabet' design.

Design size: 49 × 69 squares.

stitch count	approx. size (cm)	approx. size (in.)
11	11.5 × 16	$4\frac{1}{2} \times 6\frac{1}{2}$
14	9 × 12.5	$3\frac{1}{2} \times 5$
18	7 × 10	$2\frac{3}{4} \times 4$

Note: add 15 cm (6 in.) to each measurement for margins and turnings.
Fabric: beige aida 11 stitches to 2.5 cm (1 in.).

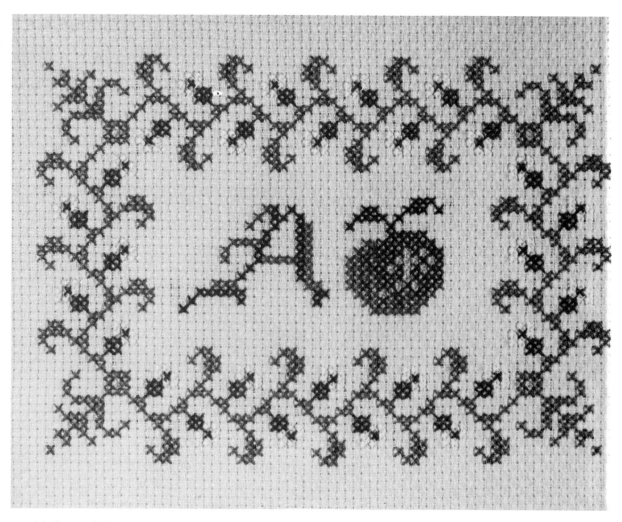

16. Cameo Letters.

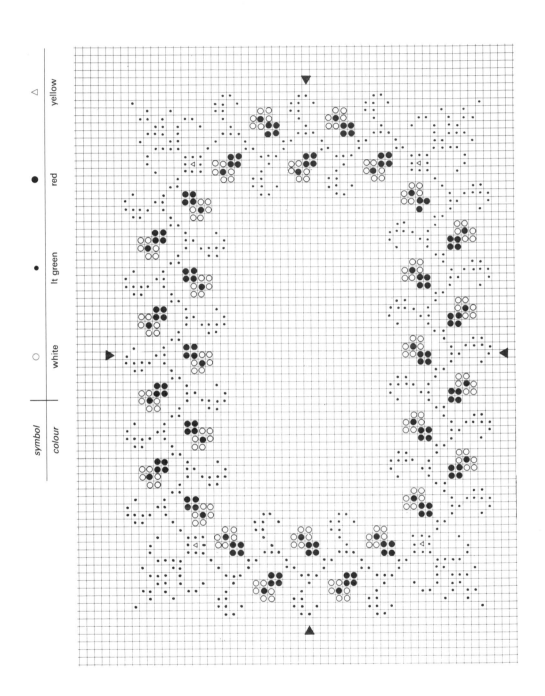

symbol	colour
△	yellow
●	red
●	lt green
○	white

African and Scandinavian Samplers

Many different countries and cultures around the world use cross stitch in their embroidery. These two samplers come from a collection of four, celebrating cultures that use variations on the cross stitch theme for decoration of their clothing and textiles. The African design includes elephants, drums and masks, while the Scandinavian has a Christmas tree, bells and cockerels. The colours are those I associate with the different cultures. Thus the Scandinavian has bright blue, red and yellow whereas the African has subtle terracotta, gold and pale blue. The borders contain appropriate motifs and patterns.

Although these designs are not very big, there is quite a lot of work in them. The borders in particular are heavily patterned and so can take some time to sew. Neither design is difficult, however, and the motifs are great fun to work. I would suggest you count out from the centre of the design to the side border. Sew the inner line of the border all the way round the design, checking with any reference lines as you sew. Once this line has been put in correctly the rest of the border will be simple to fill in. When you place the motifs, count from the border and make as many cross-references as you can.

As I have mentioned, these designs come from a set of four, the other two being an Oriental and a North American Indian sampler. If you would prefer to purchase any of the four designs with the fabric and threads already chosen and cut to size, then they can be obtained as needlework kits from Atlascraft Ltd (see page 119).

Design size (both samplers): 87 × 117 squares.

stitch count	approx. size (cm)	approx. size (in.)
11	20 × 27	$8 \times 10\frac{3}{4}$
14	16 × 21	$6\frac{1}{4} \times 8\frac{1}{2}$
18	12.5 × 16.5	$5 \times 6\frac{1}{2}$

Note: add 15 cm (6 in.) to each measurement for margins and turnings.
Fabric: white aida 11 stitches to 2.5 cm (1 in.).

Key and thread numbers (African Sampler):

symbol	●	−	•	■	○	△	□
colour	brown	beige	blue	green	gold	red	grey
Anchor	380	368	129	862	307	339	8581
DMC	839	437	809	935	783	920	646

18. Scandinavian Sampler (see also
    colour plate 8).

Key and thread numbers (Scandinavian Sampler):

symbol	●	.	■	●	—	○	▲
colour	blue	lt yellow	green	brown	beige	dk yellow	red
Anchor	132	301	210	371	368	303	11
DMC	797	676	910	435	437	742	350

symbol	colour
□	grey
◁	red
○	gold
■	green
•	blue
–	beige
●	brown

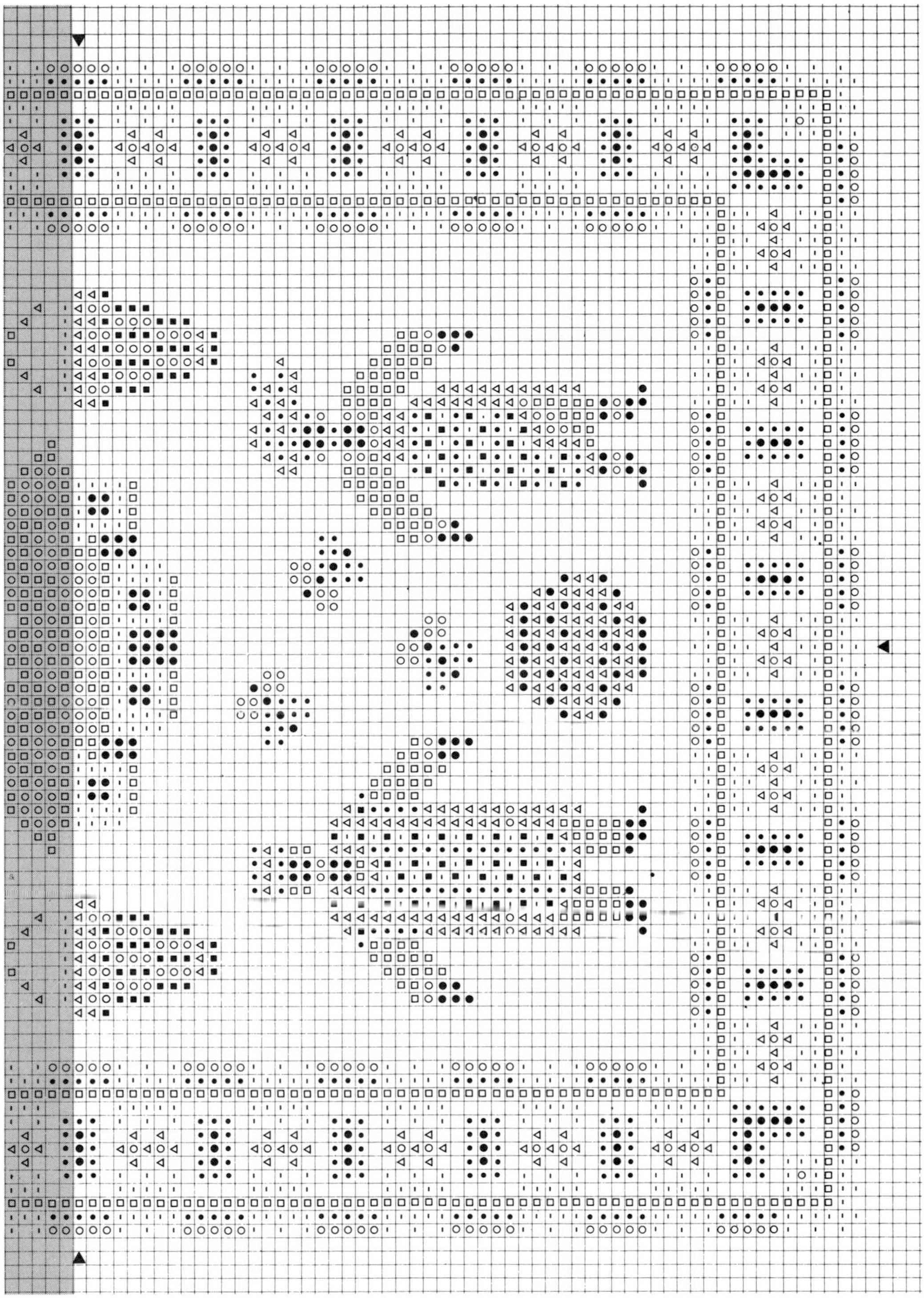

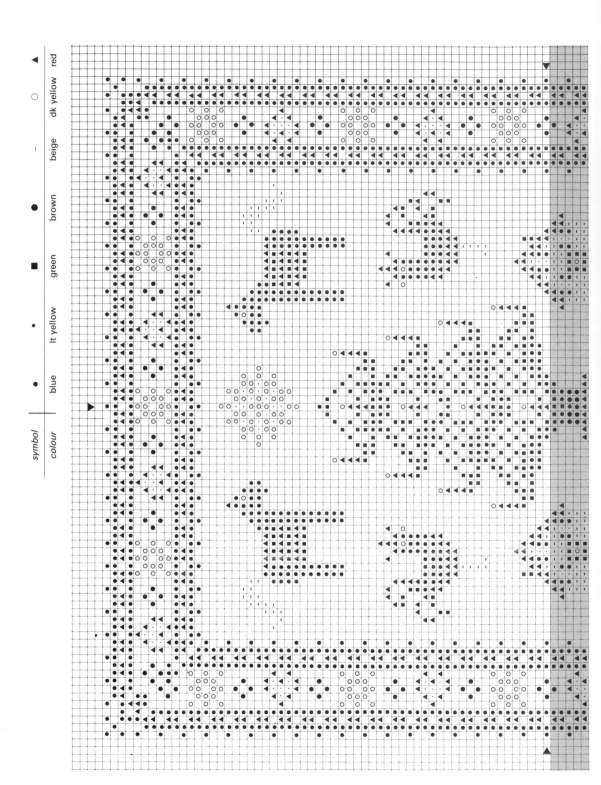

symbol	colour
◀	red
○	dk yellow
—	beige
●	brown
■	green
·	lt yellow
●	blue

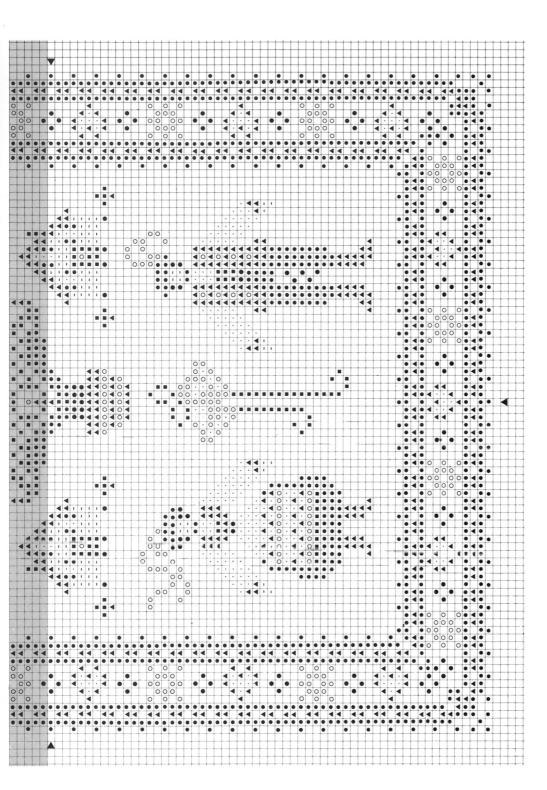

A Merry Christmas Sampler

Christmas is a traditional theme in cross stitch work, particularly in Scandinavian and European designs. Here is a bright and cheerful Christmas design which would be a pleasure both to receive and to work over the Christmas period. With Christmas cockerels, candles, presents, stockings, puddings and dolls, the sampler celebrates this very special occasion. The colours include the traditional bright red and green and are sewn on to a white fabric, making this a clear and vibrant design.

The treatment of the border is interesting as the symbols and letters are created by the fabric that is not covered with cross stitches. This is a fascinating alternative technique in the use of cross stitch, sometimes called counter-change work. If you wish to design using this technique, be aware that it is not simply a matter of drawing out a motif and then filling in the squares round it. The motifs are much more successful if they are worked out in the same way as they are to be sewn, that is, in a 'negative' form.

This is one of the few designs where I would not start by sewing the border lines. This is because the red border is made up of solid straight lines which are difficult to count and to use as reference points. Instead, sew the Christmas tree first, then the streamers and the blue horizontal line (from the bottom of the tree). Then sew the yellow inner border line. Once you have sewn these in the rest of the design should be fairly simple to relate to them. This is not a difficult design, though the less experienced embroiderer should take especial care placing the border lines in exactly the right place.

Design size: 83 × 117 squares.

stitch count	approx. size (cm)	approx. size (in.)
11	19 × 27	$7\frac{3}{4} \times 10\frac{3}{4}$
14	15 × 21	$6 \times 8\frac{1}{2}$
18	12 × 16.5	$4\frac{3}{4} \times 6\frac{1}{2}$

Note: add 15 cm (6 in.) to each measurement for margins and turnings.
Fabric: white aida 11 stitches to 2.5 cm (1 in.).

19. A Merry Christmas Sampler (see
also colour plate 9).

Key and thread numbers:

symbol	○	●	■	—	•	△
colour	yellow	green	brown	red	blue	beige
Anchor	302	879	370	13	920	372
DMC	742	500	435	349	932	739

symbol	○	●	■	–	•	△
colour	yellow	green	brown	red	blue	beige

66

67

Golden Days

This sampler was designed with the beautiful American samplers of the nineteenth century particularly in mind. The theme is a classic one and includes many traditional and familiar symbols. There are a lady and gentleman in Victorian dress walking out amidst flowers, trees and butterflies. A house in the trees, squirrels and hedgehogs, alphabet and numbers make this a suitable sampler for most people and occasions. The colours are soft and light and give the sampler a nostalgic atmosphere.

This design is a fairly complex one. There is quite a lot of detail and it will take longer to sew than some of the other samplers. You will notice that there is a mid-green line that runs through the centre of the border flowers, and which runs all the way round the design. Count out from the centre of your fabric to this line and sew this in first all the way round. Check carefully as you do this, especially with any reference lines you have marked in. Once you have sewn this line in correctly the area of the sampler will be defined, and you will have many reference points from which to work. Any of the border flowers can now be filled in, and from them it will be easy to place the line of leaves across the centre of the design, and the grass the lady and gentleman are walking on. Once these have been sewn in you should have no problems placing any of the remaining symbols.

The alphabet and numbers included within the design can be used when placing your own initials and dates. I have used the blue thread for this, but choose whichever colour you think would look best. The white thread should, wherever possible, be sewn in last to keep it clean.

Design size: 137 × 173 squares.

stitch count	approx. size (cm)	approx. size (in.)
11	31.5 × 39.5	$12\frac{1}{2} \times 15\frac{3}{4}$
14	24.5 × 31	$10 \times 12\frac{1}{2}$
18	19.5 × 24.5	$7\frac{3}{4} \times 9\frac{3}{4}$

Note: add 15 cm (6 in.) to each measurement for margins and turnings.
Fabric: ivory aida 11 stitches to 2.5 cm (1 in.).

20. Golden Days (see also colour plate 10).

Key and thread numbers:

symbol	■	●	−	△	★	▲	○	●
colour	dk green	md green	blue	white	yellow	brown	red	grey
Anchor	862	860	128	1	301	375	10	400
DMC	935	3052	800	BLANC	676	420	351	414

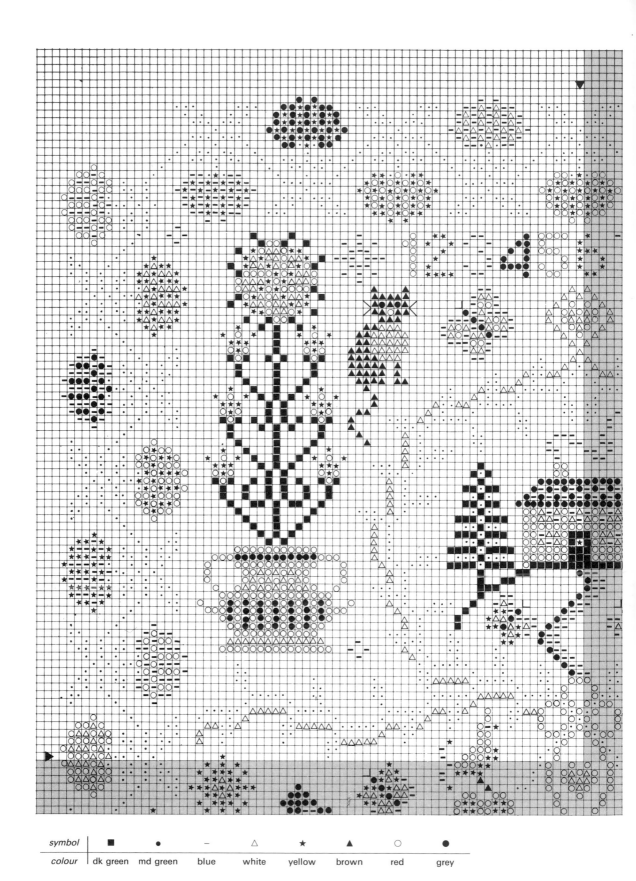

symbol	■	●	−	△	★	▲	○	●
colour	dk green	md green	blue	white	yellow	brown	red	grey

symbol	■	●	–	△	★	▲	○	●
colour	dk green	md green	blue	white	yellow	brown	red	grey

Golden Greetings

This design is an extract from the 'Golden Days' sampler and features two of the central motifs of the lady and gentleman walking among flowers and trees. The larger design is quite complex, so this smaller one might be just the thing to start on to give you the confidence to try the larger sampler.

Count out from the centre of the design to the border. Sew the mid-green line in first, as this is continuous round the whole of the design. Complete the border and refer the remaining patterns and motifs to the border.

The thread colours and colour coding are the same as those used in the main 'Golden Days' design.

Design size: 55 × 95 squares.

stitch count	approx. size (cm)	approx. size (in.)
11	12.5 × 22	$5 \times 8\frac{3}{4}$
14	10 × 17	$4 \times 6\frac{3}{4}$
18	8 × 13.5	$3\frac{1}{4} \times 5\frac{1}{2}$

Note: add 15 cm (6 in.) to each measurement for margins and turnings.
Fabric: ivory hardanger 22 stitches to 2.5 cm (1 in.), worked over two.

21. Golden Greetings.

symbol	■	●	—	△	★	◄	○	●
colour	dk green	md green	blue	white	yellow	brown	red	grey

76

3 DESIGNING CROSS STITCH SAMPLERS

No-one should be daunted at the idea of designing a sampler themselves. Just as sewing cross stitch samplers is mainly a matter of learning the correct technique and then putting in a little practice, so, with a few guidelines, designing can also be easily accomplished. As with so much design work, people find the actual starting of a design the hardest part. The problem lies in deciding what subject matter to choose (sometimes you can think of too much, at other times nothing at all will come to mind) and just how to use it. Often the possibilities seem only to confuse. One way to tackle this problem is to gather together as much material as you can. You will then have many alternatives from which to choose.

I often hear the cry: 'Oh, but I can't draw.' Well, you may be pleased to learn that it is simply not necessary to be able to draw freehand. Indeed, in some ways it can be seen as a disadvantage, as the whole aim of cross stitch design is to use stylized symbols within the squares of the fabric. The design should not, I feel, attempt to look 'realistic', though this is a matter of personal choice.

A sense of colour can also be developed by following a few guidelines. With a little practice and observation you will be able to put colours together with confidence. Any person, of any age, can gain a great deal of satisfaction from designing a sampler. Children often have a marvellously direct style that adults can only struggle to emulate!

You can, of course, design a sampler by sewing directly on to the fabric and make it up as you go along. However, most of this chapter deals with designing the sampler as a whole on graph paper, and then sewing it up from the chart you have created. Having designed your sampler, you may wish to refer to Chapter 1 on how to prepare and sew your design. If you already know this, then once you have completed your sampler, refer to Chapter 4 on finishing and framing.

Reference and source

Perhaps the hardest part of designing anything is knowing how and where to begin. One method to overcome this problem is to start by building up a large amount of reference material. This would include any direct reference to the subject you are celebrating and also any ideas that may appeal to you. For sampler designs the most obvious source of reference are the many old samplers that can be seen in historic houses and museums. It can also be rewarding to ask friends and relatives if they have any samplers that have been passed down the family as heirlooms. It is useful to carry a notebook so that reference material can be jotted down at the time.

When you come across a sampler, make an analysis of it. It helps to make a brief pencil (and possibly coloured pencil) sketch of the sampler with a few notes. It does not matter if you find sketching difficult; these are your notes and only you will have to be able to understand them! I have written a checklist that could be put into your notebook for future reference.

22. A sampler sewn in 1862 by Maria Ann Horobin, with verse, flowers and acorn border.

23. Sketch and analysis of the nineteenth-century sampler in Fig. 22.

Checklist

- number of stitches to 2.5 cm (1 in.);
- size and type of fabric used e.g. hardanger, evenweave, etc.;
- colour of thread and fabric;
- date when sewn and who sewed it;
- subject matter;
- description of border pattern and symbols used;
- style of lettering and numbers;
- type of framing.

Fig. 22 shows an old sampler from which a friend kindly allowed me to make a sketch and analysis (Fig. 23).

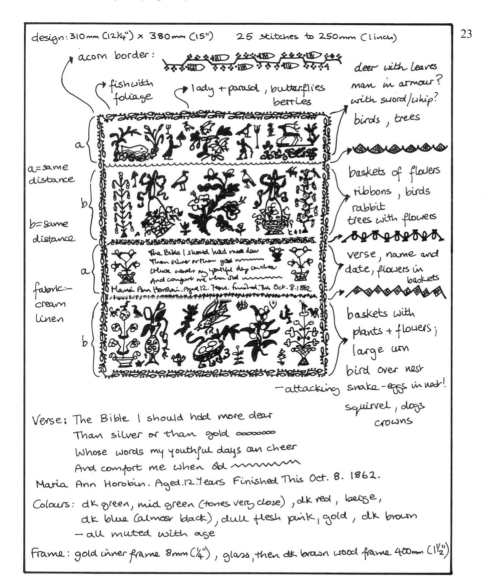

design: 310 mm (12¼") × 380 mm (15")   25 stitches to 250mm (1 inch)   23

acorn border:
deer with leaves
man in armour? with sword/whip?
birds, trees
fish with foliage
lady + parasol, butterflies berries
a = same distance
baskets of flowers
ribbons, birds
rabbit
trees with flowers
b = same distance
fabric:- cream linen
verse, name and date, flowers in baskets
baskets with plants + flowers;
large urn
bird over nest
– attacking snake – eggs in nest!
squirrel, dogs
crowns

Verse: The Bible I should hold more dear
    Than silver or than gold ooooooo
    Whose words my youthful days can cheer
    And comfort me when old ∿∿∿∿∿
Maria Ann Horobin. Aged. 12. Years Finished This Oct. 8. 1862.

Colours: dk green, mid green (tones very close), dk red, beige,
    dk blue (almost black), dull flesh pink, gold, dk brown
    – all muted with age

Frame: gold inner frame 8mm (¼"), glass, then dk brown wood frame 400mm (1½")

IF YOU YOUR LIPS WOULD KEEP FROM SLIPS
OF FIVE THINGS HAVE A CARE:
TO WHOM YOU SPEAK, OF WHOM YOU SPEAK,
AND HOW, AND WHEN, AND WHERE.

*　　*　　*

I SLEPT AND DREAMED THAT LIFE WAS BEAUTY;
I WOKE AND FOUND THAT LIFE WAS DUTY.

*　　*　　*

MARCH WINDS AND APRIL SHOWERS
BRING FORTH MAY FLOWERS.

*　　*　　*

FOURTH, ELEVENTH, NINTH AND SIXTH,
THIRTY DAYS TO EACH AFFIX;
EVERY OTHER THIRTY-ONE,
EXCEPT THE SECOND MONTH ALONE.

*　　*　　*

TIMES CHANGE, AND WE CHANGE WITH THEM.

*　　*　　*

LET THOSE LOVE NOW, WHO NEVER LOV'D BEFORE;
LET THOSE WHO ALWAYS LOV'D, NOW LOVE THE MORE.

*　　*　　*

THE BETTER THE DEED, THE BETTER THE DAY.

*　　*　　*

SPEECH IS SILVER;
SILENCE IS GOLDEN.

KEEP ME LIKE THE APPLE OF THINE EYE,
HIDE ME IN THE SHADOW OF THY WINGS.

*   *   *

THE HEAVENS DECLARE THE GLORY OF GOD,
AND THE FIRMAMENT SHEWETH HIS HANDYWORK.

*   *   *

A MERRY HEART MAKETH A CHEERFUL COUNTENANCE.

*   *   *

A LITTLE SLEEP, A LITTLE SLUMBER,
A LITTLE FOLDING OF THE HANDS IN REST.

*   *   *

WISDOM IS BETTER THAN RUBIES.

*   *   *

A WORD FITLY SPOKEN IS LIKE
APPLES OF GOLD IN PICTURES OF SILVER.

*   *   *

VIRTUE IS ITS OWN REWARD.

*   *   *

PUT NOT YOUR TRUST IN PRINCES.

*   *   *

ENOUGH IS AS GOOD AS A FEAST.

*   *   *

THY WORD IS A LAMP TO GUIDE MY FEET,
AND A LIGHT ON MY PATH.

The type of reference discussed so far is all based on existing cross stitch work. However, a great deal of material may be culled from your own imagination and by learning to look around and see whatever might lend itself to embroidery. Sketch or write down any subject, idea or object that you think may have possibilities.

For example, if you visit a stately home you might briefly sketch the house, or perhaps some topiary or formal garden might prove suitable. Remember that, in broad terms, subjects which have straight lines, or are geometric, or which have strong silhouettes will adapt most readily to cross stitch designs. A herbaceous border, for example, would be extremely difficult to interpret into squares, but particular plants and flowers, such as carnations, strawberries etc., might well be suitable.

Little verses, mottoes or inscriptions can be jotted down whenever you see or think of them. I have included on pages 80–81 a selection that might make suitable starting points for a sampler design. Quotations from the Bible, proverbs, children's chants and traditional sayings all provide a rich source of material. However, do be aware that verses of even four lines take up a lot of room when they are sketched on to graph paper, and are best sewn on finer fabric.

Lists can also be made of subjects, events and objects which particularly apply to you. Most lists would have on them things like birds, flowers, hearts, trees and houses, but I have also designed such apparently odd subjects as bicycles, elephants, thistles and even a bathroom! Almost anything can be stylized in some way. It may help to put subjects under headings so that under 'Home Sweet Home' you might write: *cat*, *dog*, *house*, *path*, *trees*, *gate* etc. The possibilities are endless, but it does help to have some of them written down before you start a design.

Most samplers are an amalgamation of symbols that have been jotted down from existing samplers, and symbols designed from scratch. In Chapter 5 you will find some borders, symbols, alphabets and numbers which can perhaps be used as a starting point. There is also some blank graph paper which can be used to jot down a few of your own ideas.

Colour

Before you start designing a particular sampler, get a general idea of the size and type of fabric you wish to use, and the sort of colour range you would like. However, be prepared to change your mind, since as you design other ideas will come to you. Choosing the colours is extremely important, and deserves a great deal of time and attention. There are a large number of different fabrics and threads to choose from, some of which are discussed and illustrated in Chapter 1.

In your notebook you may have a record of old samplers and the colours that were used. There are also many colour combinations that can be seen around you. Make a note of these and try to be consciously aware of which colours work well together and why. Photographs of colours in, say, tree bark, brick walls and fabric could also be added to your notebook. Magazine pictures can be cut out for reference, and postcards collected. Choosing and learning about colour is very rewarding, and can be greatly improved with observation and practice. When you have collected the reference material, try to analyse which colours look good together.

It is most important to remember that colours have an effect on each other. For example, a pink and a blue and the same pink and a yellow may work well together, but check that the yellow and the blue will work if sewn next to each other. Think not only of colours toning together, but consider colours which contrast well. If you choose a selection of colours that have exactly the same tonal range, the final design may look a little 'flat'. To prevent this, try including a couple of colours to contrast with, and thus lift, the other colours.

There are 'rules' on colour, but I feel that these can impose limitations more than they help. I am sure that these guidelines and suggestions will be more satisfactory in the long run, especially as colour is so much a matter of personal taste. In time I hope you will become adventurous and start experimenting with small pieces of work using, say, just two or three unusual colours together.

Drawing up

The principal ingredients in a design are its form, content and colour. Having assembled a body of reference material, the next stage is to attempt to put pencil to paper. Again, this is a stage that many people find difficult, but once a start has been made it will become easier. It is not at all necessary to be able to draw freehand to be able to design cross stitch samplers, as the emphasis will be on close observation, stylization and an appreciation of pattern. It is a mistake to try to make the symbols look realistic. Try instead to capture the essence of the subject matter. Sometimes it is best to design straight on to the graph paper rather than get side-tracked by trying to draw a subject freehand.

Once you have decided on the subject for your sampler (even if that subject is 'general'), write a list of all the things associated with it. Then do 'scribble' drawings of the various components and of the whole design. This should be very roughly drawn and must be seen simply as a starting point. Do not try to create a beautifully balanced, complete design to begin with, as you will only be disappointed later. The design process is a growing one, where each step leads to the next.

You will need few and inexpensive materials when designing your sampler:

- some rough paper for the 'scribble' sketches;
- pencils and coloured pencils/felt tips;
- eraser;
- graph paper (suitable sizes are 2 mm, 3 mm, $\frac{1}{10}$ in., $\frac{1}{8}$ in. 1 mm is too small to work on. Buy large sheets such as A1 or A2 to fit the complete design);
- ruler;
- sticky tape or drawing pins.

Secure the graph paper to a flat surface. Decide from your sketches whether you would like the sampler to be 'portrait' or 'landscape' (tall or broad) in shape. Decide very roughly what size you would like the design to be, and lightly mark this on the graph paper. You may wish to refer to the later section on calculations to help you decide the size to work to. Rule the centre stitch lines. When marking the centre, remember to mark off a whole square in the centre and not just a line (see the Practice Sampler). When counting, count from this centre stitch line. I find it easiest to begin a design using just pencil and different symbols to denote different colours.

Place any important lettering or numbers and main symbols first. Work out the border designs and other symbols on separate pieces of paper, and then transfer them to the main design. Naturally, a great deal of altering and revision will need to be done so that the final design is well balanced. You can use a coloured pencil to distinguish more clearly between stitches, but do not think too much about colour at this stage. Try to get the form and content right first. When you begin designing samplers, place symbols symmetrically, as random symbols are much harder to balance effectively.

It is often advisable to start with a subject and scale that is fairly unambitious before going on to something more complex. Good subjects to start with include sets of numbers and letters, simple borders, and simple repeated patterns or symbols. Simplicity and repetition are often more effective than large, crowded, over-colourful designs.

Having got the sampler design to a fairly ordered state in pencil and decided on the principal symbols, lettering and border, then start to differentiate the colours by using the coloured pencils or felt tips. It will not matter that the colours do not exactly match the threads, as the aim is to see which colours are next to each other. This will also help when sewing up.

Calculations!

When designing your sampler you will find that counting and calculations become part of the process. If you do not do your basic sums you may end up with some unexpected results. However, the number of calculations can be kept to the absolute minimum.

You will see from the examples in the tables that an awareness of how various factors interrelate can give much greater flexibility in the designing of your sampler. There are three basic variables when designing a sampler. These are the stitch count of the fabric, the size of the design, and the size of the frame.

To begin with, let us examine the relationship between the design and the fabric. As has been explained in previous chapters, the size of the finished design depends on the fabric. Thus, if the Practice Sampler was put on to various fabrics with different stitch counts, the calculation and result would be as in Table 2. From this you will see that if you decide at the outset which fabric you wish to use, you can calculate how large a design you will have. Always round your results up to the nearest convenient measurement, as it is always safer to calculate for slightly too much fabric than for too little.

Table 2: Calculation to determine the size of the 'Practice Sampler' on fabrics with different stitch counts

Design size: 95 × 143 squares.

stitch count	calculation (cm)	calculation (in.)	approx. design size
11	$\frac{95}{11} \times 2.5$	$\frac{95}{11}$	22 cm/8¾ in.
	$\frac{143}{11} \times 2.5$	$\frac{143}{11}$	32.5 cm/13 in.
14	$\frac{95}{14} \times 2.5$	$\frac{95}{14}$	17 cm/7 in.
	$\frac{143}{14} \times 2.5$	$\frac{143}{14}$	25.5 cm/10¼ in.
18	$\frac{95}{18} \times 2.5$	$\frac{95}{18}$	13.5 cm/5½ in.
	$\frac{143}{18} \times 2.5$	$\frac{143}{18}$	20 cm/8 in.

Of course you can just sew your design and then have a frame made (or make one yourself) to fit. However, if you have an antique frame, or a kit frame that you wish to use for a sampler, then you will need to do another calculation. For example, if you had a frame that was 30 cm × 45 cm (12 in. × 18 in.) in size, and you decided to have margins all round of about 2.5 cm (1 in.), the design size would be 25 cm × 40 cm (10 in. × 16 in.). On the various different fabrics you would have, accordingly, varying numbers of squares to design to. The calculations and results would be as shown in Table 3.

Always change the number of squares available to an odd number, so that you have a central stitch, rather than a line.

These calculations are not difficult and will help you to understand the relationships between various different factors. They can be very useful when starting a design as they help you to make some of the initial decisions.

Table 3. Calculation to show the number of squares available on different fabrics for the one required size

Required design size: 25 cm × 40 cm (10 in. × 16 in.).

stitch count	calculation (cm)	calculation (in.)	squares available
11	$\frac{25}{2 \cdot 5} \times 11$	10 × 11	110 × 176
	$\frac{40}{2 \cdot 5} \times 11$	16 × 11	
14	$\frac{25}{2 \cdot 5} \times 14$	10 × 14	140 × 224
	$\frac{40}{2 \cdot 5} \times 14$	16 × 14	
18	$\frac{25}{2 \cdot 5} \times 18$	10 × 18	180 × 288
	$\frac{40}{2 \cdot 5} \times 18$	16 × 18	

Note: always change the number of squares available to an odd number so that you have a central stitch line to design around.

The Practice Sampler

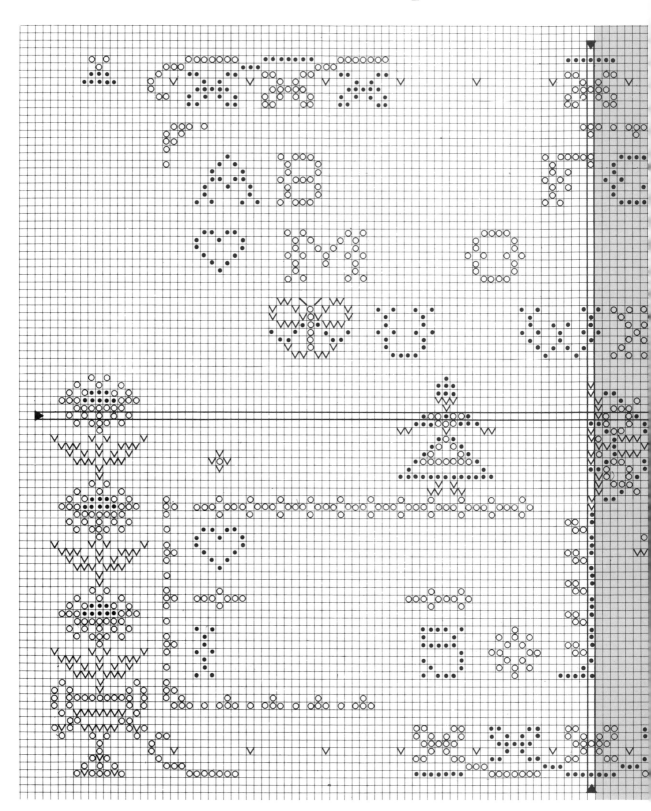

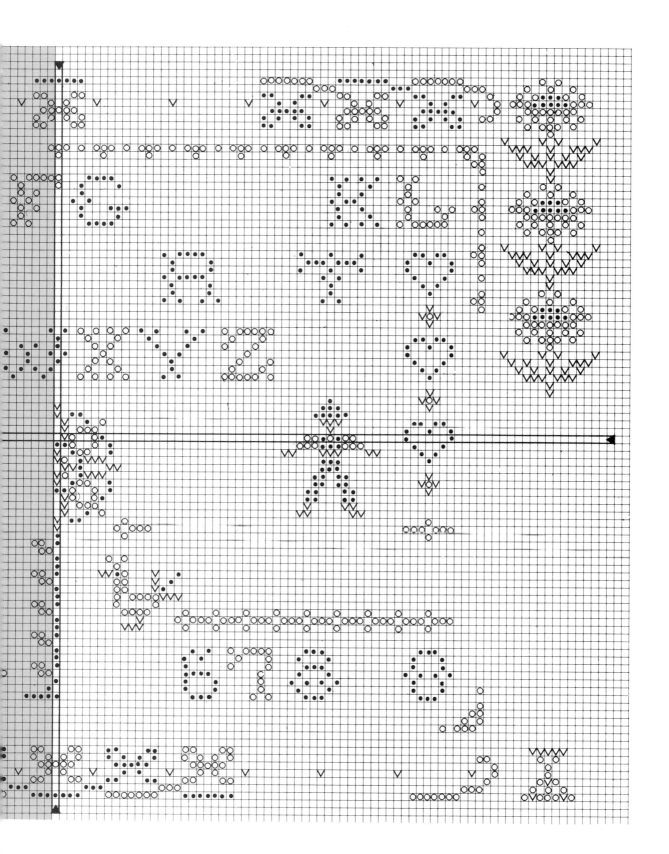

On pages 86–7 I have charted up part of a sampler design for you to complete. At present it looks a little like a confusing 'dot-to-dot' puzzle, but by completing the borders and copying out the symbols you will gain a working knowledge of the procedure to follow when designing your own sampler. One advantage you will also find when designing and drawing up your own design is that it will become so familiar that the sewing of it will be much easier.

When you start to complete the Practice Sampler I would suggest you begin by sketching in the inner border line, and the horizontal lines. The remaining alphabet and numbers are to be found in the reference section. Leave two spaces between each letter. Fill in the other half of the tree and place the remaining hearts. The man, woman, butterfly and bird simply repeat themselves, reversed on the opposite sides. There is room for your name and date in the space between the horizontal lines (by the time you have got this far it should be obvious!). Consult Chapter 1 about how to place initials and date if you do not already know how to do so.

I have used three different symbols when charting up this part-design. These symbols do not represent any particular colours but are simply a means of identifying one section of a pattern from another. If you wish to make up this design, you should choose your own colours. If you have not already read the section on colour I would recommend that you do so before choosing your fabric and threads. I would suggest you do not use more than five colours (or even less) and combine similar tones of colours. The previous section on calculations shows how different fabrics will affect the size of design (Table 2).

4 FINISHING AND FRAMING

When you have finished sewing your sampler (whether it is one taken from this book or one you have designed yourself), it will be creased though (I hope) clean. Remove any small pieces of dirt and fluff using sticky tape. Press small lengths of tape gently on the front and back of the design until it looks clean. If necessary, trim any threads on the back so that it is neat and tidy.

If your sampler has got very dirty while it was being sewn, then it can be washed. First check that the threads and fabric you have used are colourfast. Then, using gentle soap flakes, wash it carefully in lukewarm water. Rinse and dry flat. Before it is completely dry, either iron or stretch it as described in the next section. (Under no circumstances attempt to wash an antique sampler!)

Ironing or stretching

Stretching your sampler will take longer, but it does give a good finish. However, ironing will be quite adequate. If you decide to iron your sampler you will need two clean cloths (preferably white cotton fabric), and a towel. Place the sampler face down on the towel which has been covered with a cloth. Dampen the other cloth and lay it on top of the sampler. Iron lightly with a fairly hot iron. Ironing on a towel helps to push the stitches out from the fabric, rather than pressing them in.

If you decide to have your sampler framed by a picture framer then they will stretch it for you. It is quite possible to do this yourself, however, and achieve a very good finish. You will need:

- soft pin board;
- drawing pins (thumb tacks);
- white cotton fabric to cover the board;
- a straight edge and right angle (e.g. a set square);
- tape measure.

Cover the board with the cloth and damp it to make sure the board will not stain through the cloth. Leave it to dry overnight. Clean the front and back of the sampler as described, and place it right side up on the board. Starting at the middle of one side, pin the fabric down, stretching it sideways as it is pinned. Work out evenly from the centre (Fig. 24). Then pin the opposite side in the same way, but stretch the fabric both across and sideways (Fig. 25).

24

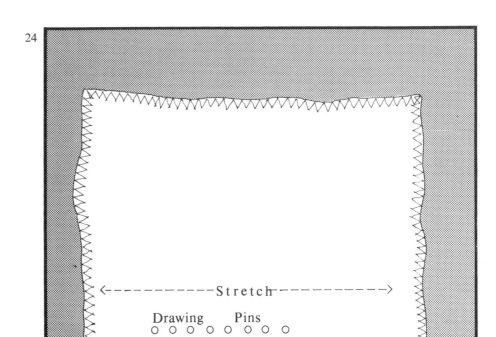

<−−−−−−−−−−−−−−−Stretch−−−−−−−−−−−−−−−−>

Drawing   Pins
○ ○ ○ ○   ○ ○ ○ ○

25

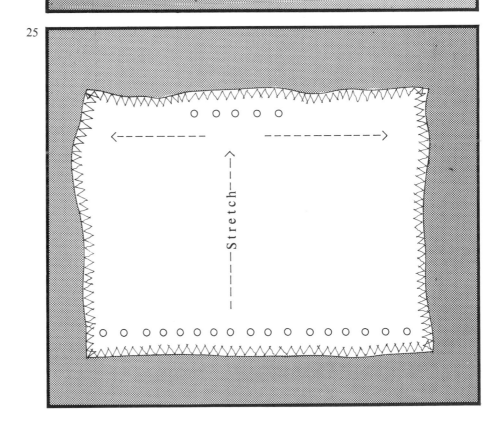

Pin the remaining two sides in the same manner (Fig. 26). Check that the lines of the sampler are straight and square by using the set square and tape measure (Fig. 27). You may well find that you have to unpin a whole side and repin it all the way round before you get the design absolutely taut and square.

Spray with water from a plant or clothes spray, or use a sponge. The sampler needs to be thoroughly damp, but not wringing wet. Leave it in a warm place such as an airing cupboard until it is completely dry.

Stringing

Whatever type of frame you decide to use, I would recommend that you back your sampler on to strong white card (or even white-painted hardboard). You do not have to use white card, but if you use a darker colour such as a grey, the fabric will appear more textured. It is a matter of experimenting and deciding which effect you prefer. The advantage of stringing your sampler over card (rather than, say, sticking it with masking tape) is that you can get it taut and positioned in the right place.

24. Stretching the first side of a sampler.

25. Stretching the opposite side.   26. Stretching the remaining two sides.

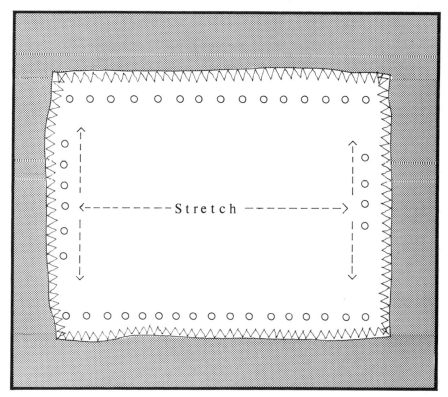

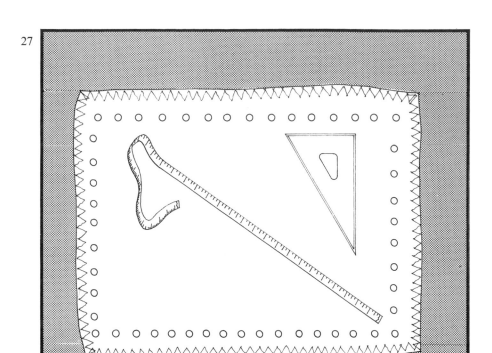

27

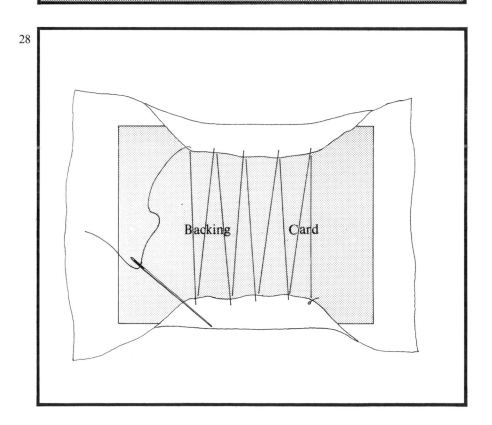

28

For the stringing you will need:

- backing card (strong white);
- sharp cutting/modelling knife;
- edge to cut against (e.g. metal ruler);
- strong thread;
- strong needle.

If you decide to frame the sampler yourself, it is usually best to get the frame section, glass and hardboard backing cut to size before you cut the backing card. This is because the backing card needs to be the same size as the glass. Cut the backing card with the sharp knife and metal ruler. Place the stretched sampler face down on a clean surface. Then place the backing card white side down on the sampler.

Take the needle and a long piece of thread and secure it in the centre of one of the long sides. Sew backwards and forwards until both edges have been pulled tightly over the card. Sew about 1 cm ($\frac{1}{2}$ in.) in from the edge of the fabric, and make the intervals no larger than 2 cm ($\frac{3}{4}$ in.) (Fig. 28).

When you have finished these sides, check that the sampler has been evenly

27. Checking the sampler has been stretched straight and square.

28. Stringing the long sides of a sampler over strong card.

29. Stringing the two shorter sides.

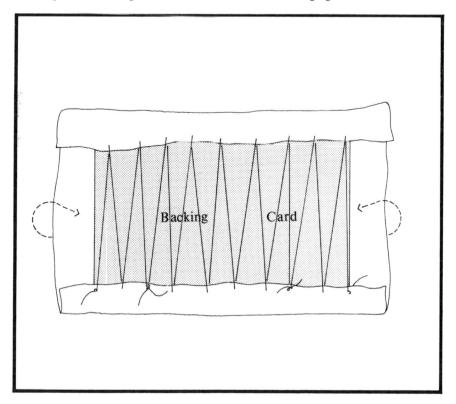

Backing   Card

placed as you wish on the card. Bear in mind that a picture often looks better if the bottom margin is slightly larger than the top and sides. Because the sampler is not actually fixed, you should be able to ease it over the card if you need to adjust the positioning.

String the short sides, working from the centres as before (Fig. 29). When it is finished, the fabric should have been pulled taut over the card and be correctly positioned (Fig. 30).

Window mounts

If you decide to put a cardboard mount round your sampler, take the sampler with you when selecting the card, so that they will complement one another. Choosing the colour of the mounting card is not easy, and care needs to be taken to ensure that the card and the sampler balance each other. I tend not to use mounts if the sampler is fairly large, as I think it may look more authentic without. However, I do use them for smaller designs, as I find they help to emphasize the picture.

You can cut the mount yourself with the sharp knife and rule, but if you want nice bevelled edges it is best taken to a picture framer to be cut. Many framers will cut just mounts if you give them the appropriate measurements. In Fig. 31 **X** and **Y** should be the same size as the glass size. The distances of **a**, **b**, **c** and **d** must also be given, though the mount often looks better if **d** is deeper than **a**, **b** or **c**.

Framing

There are many books written on the various methods and styles of picture framing. For a full account it may help to refer to one of these. I shall simply give an example of how to make a good frame with the minimum amount of skill. You can, of course, take your sampler to a picture framer, but it may prove expensive, and it would be worth while looking round at all the different framing sections before you make up your mind.

It is possible to cut and mitre all the various pieces needed for the frame yourself. However, this is really quite difficult, and I have found it better to enlist the help of a friendly picture framer or DIY shop, who will cut the pieces for you to assemble. Firstly you will need to select your framing section. There are many different ones to choose from, though I tend to prefer small light frames for samplers (Fig. 32). When choosing the framing, take the sampler with you so that you can compare them and see that they go well together.

You will need to tell the framer the section and the size you want it cut to. This is the glass size (that is, the size of the inside of the frame rebate).

30. The finished strung sampler.

31. Measurements to be decided for a window mount.

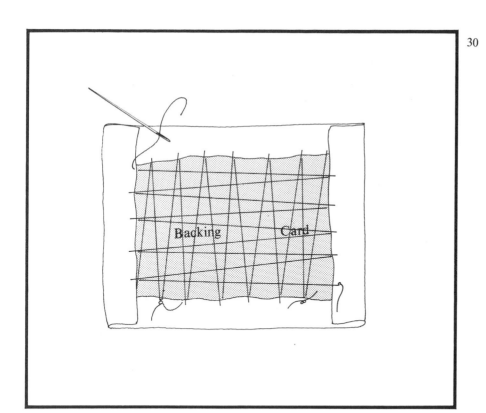

30

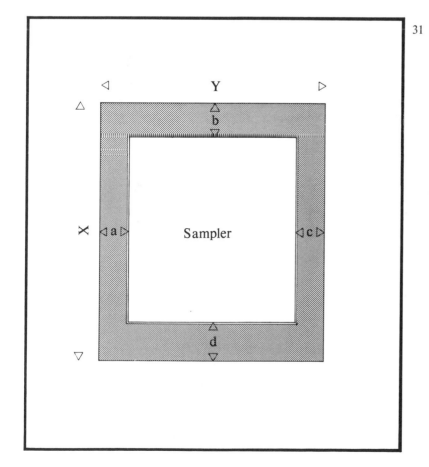

31

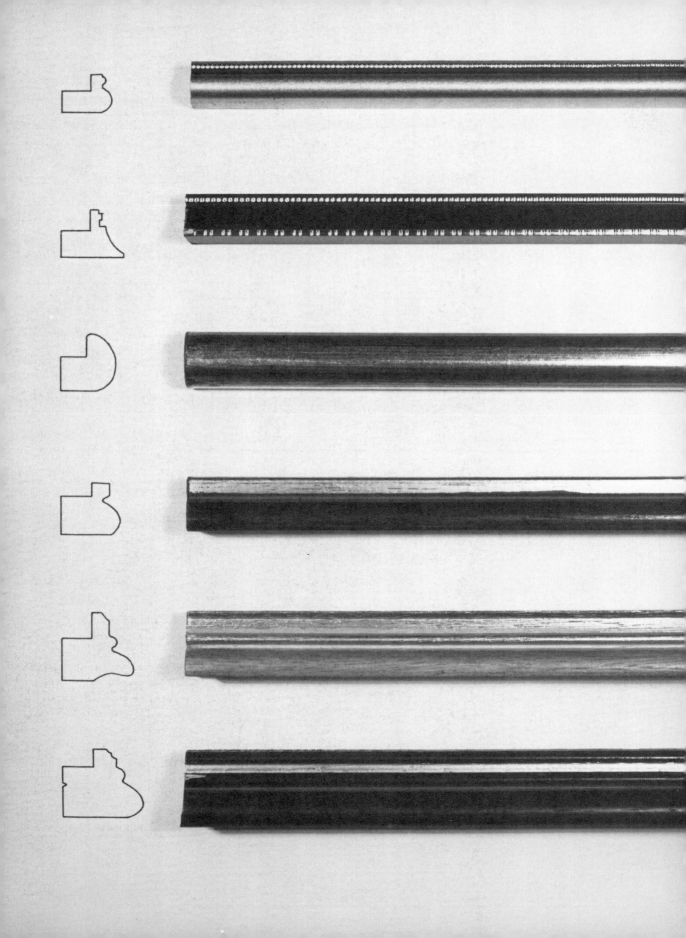

Ask the framer to provide you with:

- mitred section, cut to length;
- thin hardboard backing, cut to size;
- 2 mm glass cut to size (reflective or non-reflective, as you prefer);
- picture hooks;
- picture cord;
- stapler (staple gun), panel pins;
- strong wood glue, rapid or impact adhesive;
- picture clamps or string;
- masking tape, brown gummed tape or brown paper.

Glue and assemble the mitred lengths. Either tie the string round the frame to hold the joints tight, or use picture clamps (the plastic ones are not very expensive and are a good investment if you think you may make several frames) (Fig. 33). Check that the glass and backing will fit the frame when the

32. Selection of light framing suitable
    for samplers.

33. Assembling the frame sections using
    plastic picture clamps.

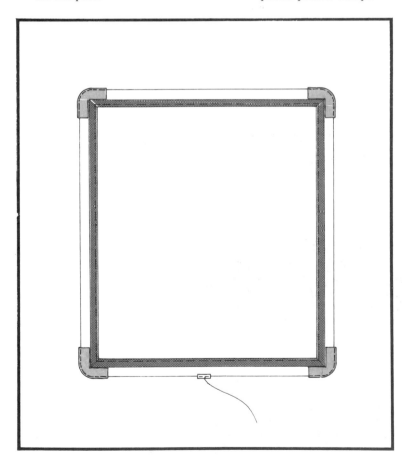

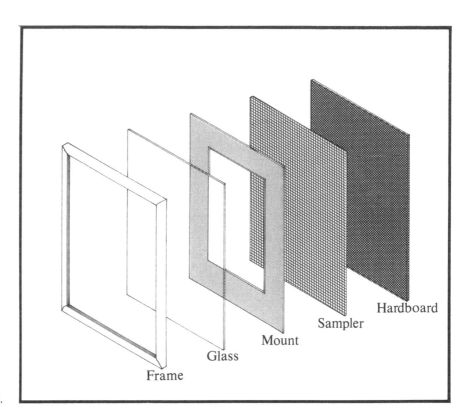

34. Order of final assembly.

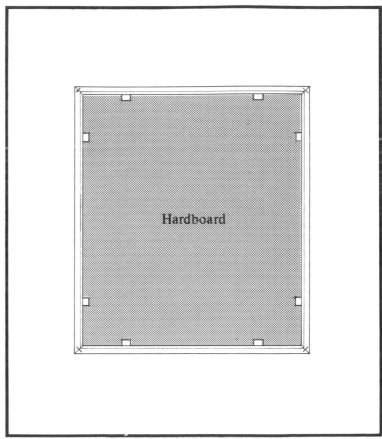

Hardboard

35. Securing the backing board.

final assembly is done. When the glue is completely dry, staple across the corners, or tap in panel pins using great care.

Clean one side of the glass and place it, clean side inside, in the frame. Place the cardboard window mount on the glass if you are using one. Make sure that your sampler, by now mounted and strung, is absolutely clean. Then place it in the frame (Fig. 34).

Before fixing the backing, just lift up all the layers to make sure no dirt has got in between the glass and picture. Then secure the backing board with staples or panel pins tapped into the frame (Fig. 35).

Put masking tape all the way round, covering the gap between backing and frame. Use brown gummed tape, or brown paper as you wish. Measure down from the top edge a few centimetres on either side, and screw in the picture hooks. Finally, string the picture cord through the hooks and neaten the ends by singeing (do a test piece first!). Clean the front of the glass, and you should have a neat and smart frame for your sampler.

Though these instructions may seem involved, you will find that making your own frame is not complicated at all. Once you have found that you can present your sampler in this way, it will encourage you to sew more designs!

5 REFERENCE

I have charted out for you a selection of different cross stitch designs, including borders, alphabets, motifs of plants and trees, figures and many more symbols that you might like to use when designing your own samplers. If you decide to include any of them it helps to count up and find out how many squares the symbol occupies. Then refer to the space you wish to fill and make sure it will fit before you transfer it to your design.

The various symbols used in coding the reference charts simply outline or differentiate areas of colour. They do not refer to any colour in particular.

At the end of this section you will find some pages of graph paper on which you can design your own patterns and motifs.

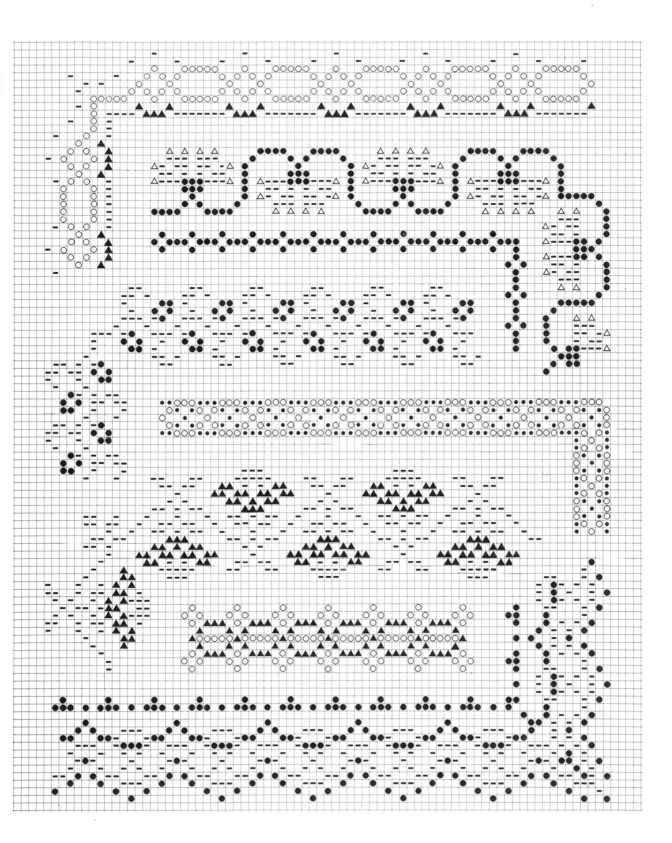

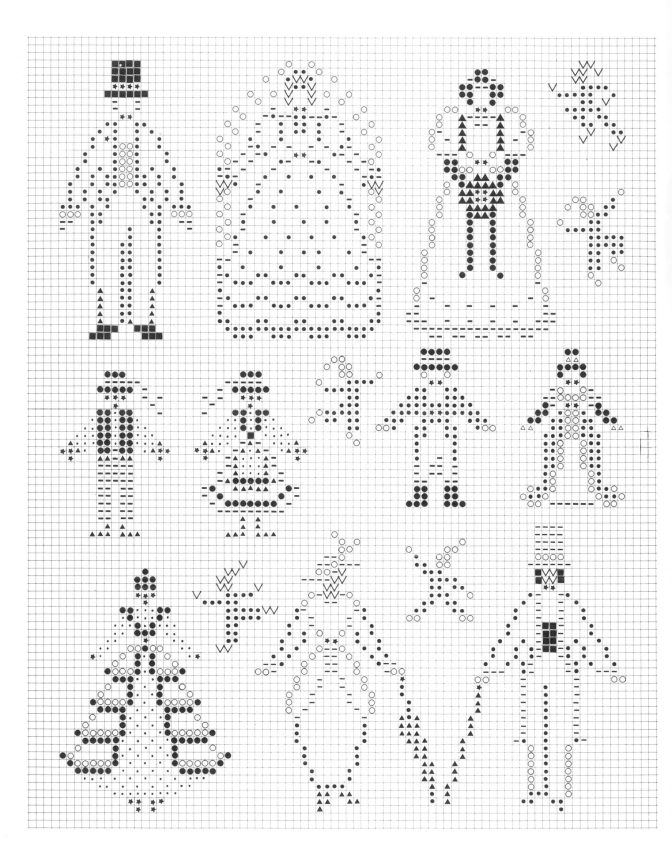

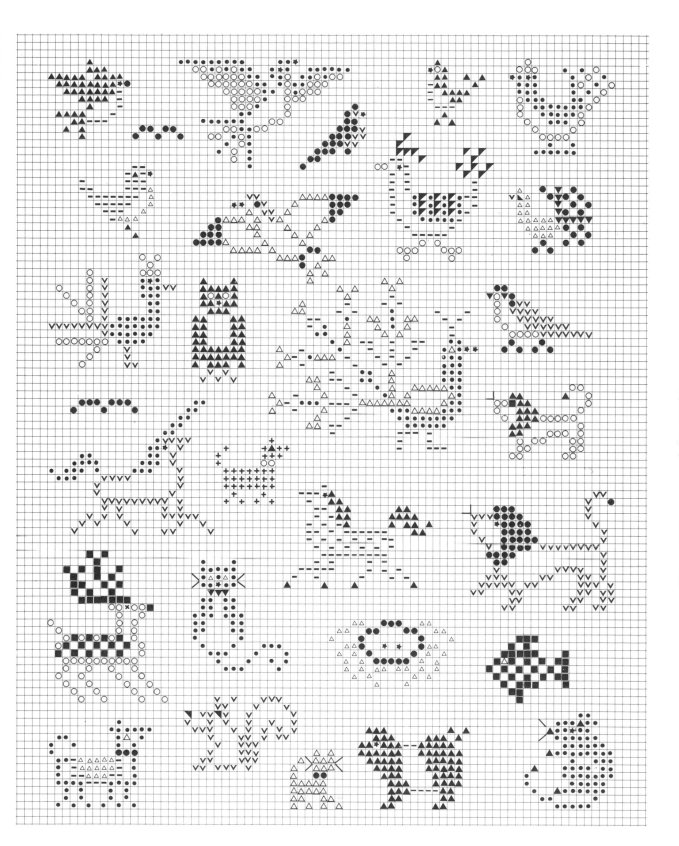

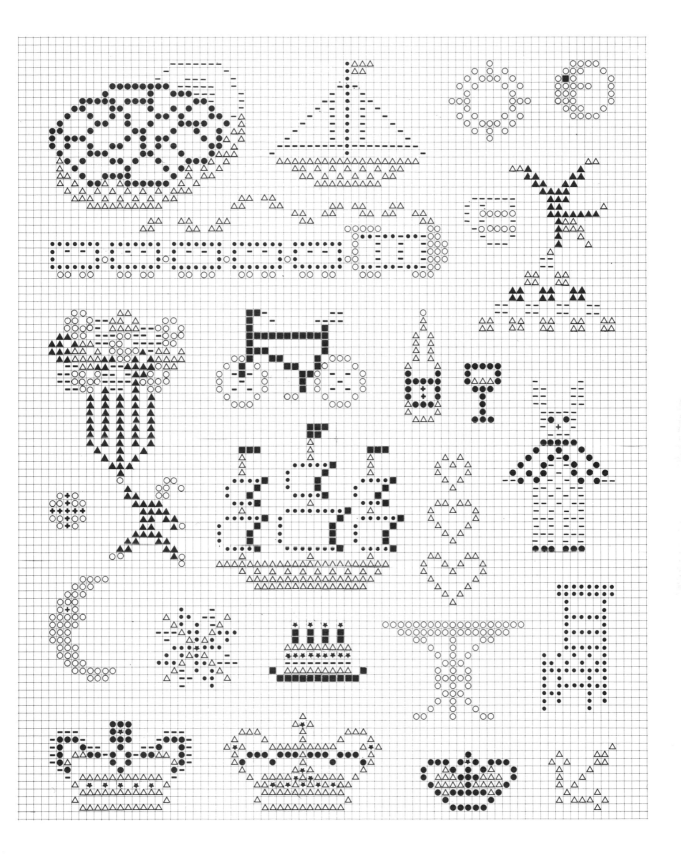

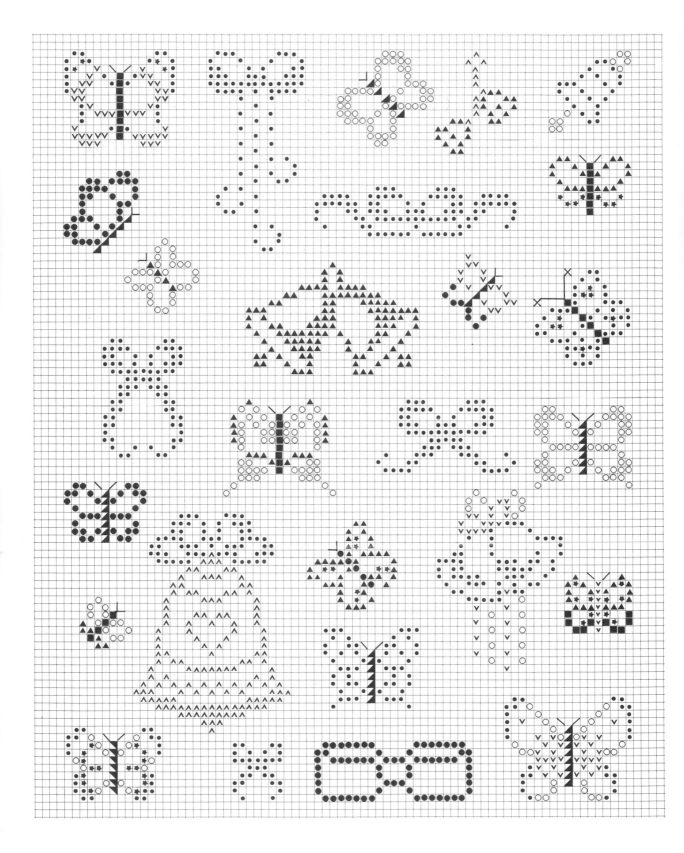

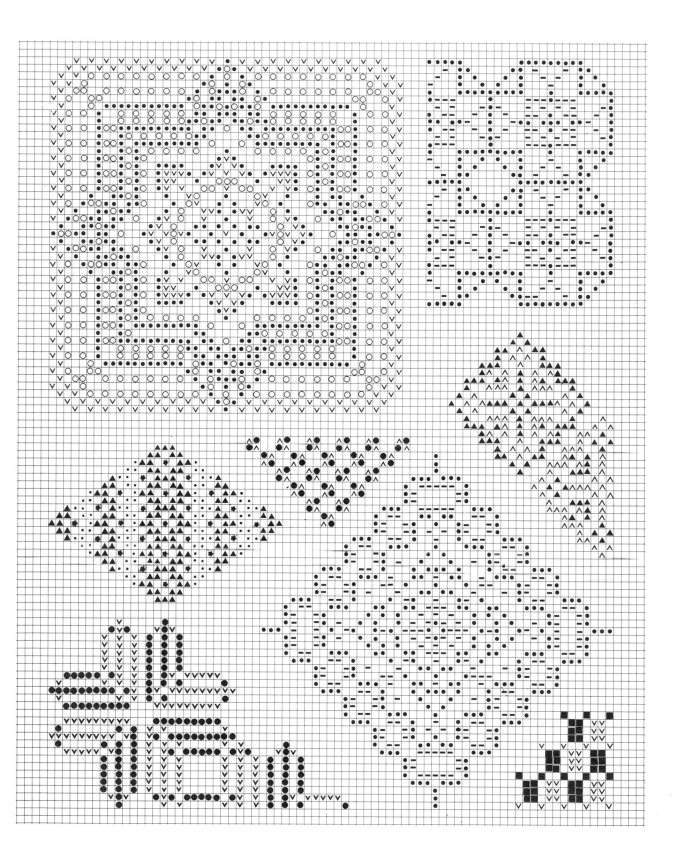

Bibliography

CHRISTIE, Mrs A., *Samplers and Stitches*, Batsford 1920, 1985.

CLABBURN, P., *Samplers*, Shire Publications Ltd 1977.

COLBY, A., *Samplers*, Batsford 1964, 1984.

FAWDRY, M. and BROWN, D., *The Book of Samplers*, Lutterworth Press 1980.

GIERL, Irmgard, *Cross Stitch Patterns*, Batsford 1977.

KING, D., *Samplers*, Victoria & Albert Museum (HMSO) 1960.

MEULENBELT-NIEUWBURG, A., *Embroidery Motifs from Dutch Samplers*, Batsford 1974, 1984.

RUSSELL, P., *Lettering for Embroidery*, Batsford 1971, 1985.

WOODS, M., *Mounting and Framing Pictures*, Batsford 1978, 1981.

Suppliers

UK

For cross stitch needlework kits:
Atlascraft Ltd
17 Ludlow Hill Road
Melton Road
West Bridgford
Nottingham NG2 6HD

For Paterna Persian Yarn:
NeedleArt House
Albion Mills
Wakefield WF2 9SG

For materials generally:
Mace and Nairn
89 Crane Street
Salisbury
Wiltshire SP1 2PY

The Nimble Thimble
26 The Green
Bilton
Rugby CV22 7LY

Christine Riley
53 Barclay Street
Stonehaven
Kincardineshire AB3 2AR

Royal School of Needlework
25 Princes Gate
London SW7 1QE

USA

For materials generally:
Appleton Bros of London
West Main Road
Little Compton
Rhode Island 02837

Bucky King Embroideries
Box 371
King Bros
3 Ranch Buffalo Star Rte
Sheridan
Wyoming 82801

The Golden Eye
Box 205
Chestnut Hill
Massachusetts 02167

The Thread Connection
Center for the Needle Arts
1020 East Carson Street
Pittsburgh
Pennsylvania 15203

Companies in the USA who will supply lists of stockists of their products

For Paterna Yarn:
Johnson Creative Arts Inc.
West Townsend
Massachusetts 01474

For Anchor thread (also known as Susan Bates/Anchor):
Susan Bates Inc.
PO Box E
Route 9A
212 Middlesex Ave
Chester
Connecticut 06412

For DMC thread:
The DMC Corporation
107 Trumbell Street
Elizabeth
New Jersey 07206

119

Index